THE ONES THAT GOT AWAY

The misadventures of an outdoor writer

by Steve Grooms

Willow Creek Press

Copyright ©1992 Steve Grooms
Published by Willow Creek Press
An imprint of NorthWord Press, Inc.
P.O. Box 1360
Minocqua, WI 54548

Edited by Greg Linder
Designed by Russell S. Kuepper
Illustrations by Bruce Cochran

Library of Congress Cataloging-in-Publication Data

Grooms, Steve.
    The ones that got away / [Steve Grooms].
      p. cm.
    ISBN 1-55971-181-7: $9.95
    I. Title.
PN6231.S65G76 1992
796'.0207--dc20   92-24545
                                              CIP

DEDICATION

This one's for Kathe.

TABLE OF CONTENTS

Introduction

What follows is a collection of stories arising from the experiences of one outdoor sportsman. For better or worse—and generally speaking, it is for worse—the stories are true. In fact, they are not even exaggerated, at least not much.

Some of these stories are sweet and reflective. They give me no trouble. But others, the "funny" stories, bother me. In fact, I anticipate the publication of this book with a mixture of pride and dread. Why? Why do I quiver with fear as my new book goes to press? At the bottom of it, seems to me, I'm afraid somebody might actually read these stories.

And what will they see? They'll see *me* . . . go-go dancing in my deer stand. *Me* experiencing the worst slump in the history of fishing. *Me* freaking out after hooking a bat while fly fishing in the dark. *Me* getting crapped on in the face by a pigeon when . . .

Well, it just goes on and on.

This isn't your ordinary selection of outdoor hero stories. Our Hero goes in pursuit of steelhead on a wilderness stream and somehow lands in Ontario's sleaziest bar watching a truly remarkable performance by Canada's toughest stripper. Our Hero goes deer hunting and nearly passes out with fear on his tree stand.

This isn't even your ordinary selection of outdoor humor stories. Patrick McManus and Joel Vance tell stories that feature their ineptness, but readers know better. They know that stuff is fiction. They know that McManus can actually handle a canoe, just as Vance is a pretty good quail hunter.

Not Steve Grooms. When I write that I fished thirteen days in a row without even catching a cold, readers will know it is true. Coming from me, such a statement will be credible.

I really don't understand why I am doing this. Every outdoor sportsman has pretensions to glory. (Or at least to minimal inadequacy.) We are all the stars of our own stories. But not Our Hero. It's as if Grooms goes hunting and fishing with the crew of *Candid*

Camera in tow, so they can record his every blunder, backlash, and belch.

Worse, much worse: He patches together all these *highly* compromising bits of film in one document, a stunning testimonial to flaming incompetence and the frailties of the human spirit. And worse still: This shocking confession comes from someone who has had the unmitigated gall to make his living telling other sportsmen how to hunt and fish. Which, when you think about it, is like Wiley E. Coyote writing books on the catching, cleaning, and cooking of roadrunners. So why, why have I gone to such *pains* to show myself as an utterly inept ass?

I don't know. Maybe it is because I'm not clever enough to lie. Maybe it is because I am clever enough to know that pretending to expertise is an unpromising enterprise, given the material I have to work with. Maybe it is because I think most sportsmen would breathe a little easier (and be nicer to live with) if outdoor writers spiced up their copy with occasional dashes of candor. Maybe it is because I see Truth-in-Outdoor-Writing as a virgin field of literature in which even I can sell a few books by getting in on the ground floor.

I already enjoy the dubious distinction of being possibly the first outdoor writer in history to describe himself having an attack of diarrhea in the field. This incident appears in my book, *Pheasant Hunter's Harvest* (which is a pretty good book, incidentally, and no sportsman's library is complete without two or three copies of it!). Now, in this book, I describe another such incident.

If anyone ever erects a statue to commemorate Steve Grooms' contributions to outdoor literature, I know what the pose will be.

Take This Bird and Stuff It!

Back when I was a kid, the ad for the Northwest School of Taxidermy used to run just inside the front cover of the big outdoor magazines. The cartoon-style ad showed two earnest young men with heavily greased hair saying, "**Taxidermy** is the most **thrilling hobby** in the world for **men** and **boys!**" The ad claimed I could learn taxidermy "in my own time at my own workbench" if I signed up for the School's correspondence course.

I didn't have a workbench, and maybe that should have given me pause, but it didn't. I was fascinated by the process of creating art from corpses, the alchemy by which dead animals can be brought to life again.

I sent off to Omaha for the School's 44-page brochure. The brochure, which appeared to have been printed sometime around the turn of the century, was full of tales of youngsters who achieved SUCCESS through the School's program. I was assured that the School's founder, J.J. Elwood, would take a personal interest in my progress as I ascended lesson by lesson toward the mastery of taxidermy. I think there were a dozen lessons, so this was a sort of "twelve-step program."

There was a little problem about money. The course cost more than I had. I discussed that with my buddies, Nick and Mike. They chipped in a couple bucks apiece for the right to read my lesson pamphlets. I enrolled.

The first snag came when the first lesson arrived, the one called "How to Skin a Bird." I studied the pamphlet with fascination. The black-and-white sketches seemed clear enough, though they were nothing you'd want to watch while eating. I was eager to begin.

It then occurred to me that, before I could breathe life into a dead animal through the alchemy of taxidermy, I had to have a dead animal. There I was—deep in the shank of winter, with no animals "in season," and I didn't even have a gun or a car. Acquiring a dead bird wasn't going to be easy.

My pals and I chewed that one over for several days. We knew where some birds hung out. A sizable flock of pigeons lived under a railway overpass about a mile from my house. But that overpass was only two blocks from the downtown business district. We'd surely get nabbed by the town police if we hunted pigeons with firearms—or bows and arrows—so near our town's center of commerce.

So my career as a taxidermist was put on hold while we learned to make and use blowguns. Blowguns were the quietest weapon we could think of that would allow us to collect a pigeon for scientific purposes.

We made our blowguns from six-foot sections of electrical conduit. For mouthpieces, we taped on red plastic Redi-Whip aerosol-bomb tops. We made darts by cutting sections of clothes-hanger wire and wrapping them with cotton batting to form the air seal. The points didn't look lethal enough, so we soldered on wicked-looking broadheads cut from a tuna can. Our blowguns were tolerably accurate to thirty feet, though it took the lungs of a carnival barker to fire them.

Early in the hunt, distressed businessmen obviously phoned the cops to say they'd spotted juveniles loitering around the underpass with long pipes and guilty expressions, and didn't *that* look damn suspicious? The police soon gave the underpass "saturation coverage," sending a squad car through every fifteen minutes. (This was back in a more innocent time when cops had nothing better to do than chase young scientists with blowguns.)

The heavy police presence complicated a hunt that was already proving more challenging than we'd hoped. We had to time our shots for those moments when pigeons were in range and prowl cars were not. Once I ran out directly under a pigeon and took aim, but the pigeon fired first.

About this time, J.J. Elwood wrote a nice letter. As promised, he was concerned about my progress. He was sure I'd want to stuff my bird, now that I'd skinned it. He included my second lesson: "How To Mount A Bird." J.J. gently suggested I'd want to buy a few tools and materials that, by a stroke of good fortune, the

School was willing to sell me. I didn't see why I needed a surgical steel scalpel imported from Europe when I already owned a jackknife. It was just a little dull from extensive use playing mumblety-peg.

I was jolted to read that I'd be building up my bird's body with string and something called "excelsior" that the pamphlet breezily assured me I had lying around my basement. I had never seen excelsior and didn't have a clue as to what it was. Later I learned it was a shaved-wood packing material that *was* found in every household basement . . . four or five decades earlier. In the diagrams, excelsior looked like steel wool. I planned to make that substitution, though it raised the disquieting vision that my stuffed pigeon might rust.

We finally nailed a pigeon before the gendarmes could nail us. I laid him belly-up on the ping-pong table in my basement—my "workbench"—and began separating him from his skin. Somehow, this all looked neater in the diagrams. I quickly learned that I had neither the skill nor the patience for this meticulous work. All those optional tools the School was eager to sell me began to look obligatory. I began to learn the difference between a surgical steel scalpel and a dull jackknife.

I was happy to break off the project when my mother called me to lunch. When I came back, the pigeon was crawling—inside and out—with a bazillion wriggling white worms. *Yuccch!* Who wants a stuffed *pigeon* anyway?

Then, renouncing birds in general, my attention turned to a page in the School's brochure that pictured a mount I admired enormously. It featured four frogs sitting on chairs around a table, playing poker. They had little frog-sized cards, a frog-sized booze bottle on the table, and two of them smoked frog-sized stogies. I was also tempted by a mount pictured on the opposite page, a perky squirrel with a clock planted in his belly and an electrical cord coming out of his anus. But the frogs were funnier as they sat there with their fat little legs crossed, drinking and bullshitting the night away.

Besides, I was getting canny. A frog is smaller than a squirrel or a pigeon and would presumably take less effort to mount. And, to the best of my knowledge, frogs were totally free of wriggling white parasites.

J.J. Elwood wrote again. He was growing concerned because I hadn't sent him any pictures of my bird mount. But now, instead of being a comforting, encouraging educator, J.J. was beginning to come off as something of a nag.

Acquiring a frog proved far easier than blowgunning a pigeon, though most of the frogs we collected were a little flat for taxidermy purposes, since we used logs to club them. It was spring by then. The rutting season for frogs was going full bore at the local Izaak Walton Club lake. We were able to sneak up on quite a few lovesick frogs as they pitched woo with deep, slack-string belches.

I picked the roundest of our frogs for my second taxidermy project. To skin an amphibian, said the pamphlet, you make no cuts at all. You just turn him inside out "like a glove," removing pieces of his innards through his mouth with tweezers. That sounded easy. We even had some eyebrow tweezers in our bathroom cabinet.

I thought I was doing pretty well when, halfway through the project, I saw that my clumsy tweezer technique had enlarged the frog's mouth until it was only slightly smaller than the *opening* of a glove. While I pondered that, I saw how hard it would be to cover up my mistake with the usual taxidermy techniques. A taxidermist repairs skin cuts with stitches. But the frog had very little hair under which I could hide my stitches. And several inches worth were now needed at the corners of my frog's mouth.

I renounced frogs as I had renounced birds.

J.J. Elwood's next letter had a slightly arch tone: Hey, wasn't my bird done yet? And how was I coming on my amphibian? He sent me instructions for mounting a fish. One glance at these instructions made it clear that it would be a waste of time for me to even try a fish. Even the irritatingly optimistic J.J. admitted fish weren't easy.

Growing desperate, I turned to mammals—they had hair to hide the stitches. Once again, my development as a taxidermist was delayed, while my buddies and I worked out a way of collecting a suitable animal to mount. It was now fall.

We decided to try for a raccoon because we were impressed by a picture in the brochure showing a mounted raccoon washing a crayfish in a plaster-of-Paris stream. None of us had ever seen a living coon, though we often found tracks in the muddy banks of nearby Squaw Creek. So coons were apparently common in our vicinity. We bought a collection of leg-hold traps and set out to trap one.

I wish I had time to tell the whole story of our trapping adventures. (*Ha! That's a damn lie! Besides, the statute of limitations ran out on all that stuff a long time ago.*) Essentially, we never came anywhere near trapping a raccoon, which is a pretty intelligent animal—particularly as compared to three twelve-year-old wanna-be taxidermists.

We did finally catch a cottontail rabbit, which we ate rather than stuffed, plus a bizarre creature with a pointy face and naked tail. It seemed to be a juvenile of its species, which we didn't know. To identify it, we hied off to the library. We hadn't known there even *were* possums in Iowa.

Going into the possum mounting project, I sensed that this was the do-or-die point in my taxidermy career. But I couldn't see mounting the possum washing a crayfish in a plaster-of-Paris stream (and geez, how do you skin a crayfish, anyway—they have smaller mouths than frogs, even!).

Studying the lesson on mounting mammals raised a number of concerns. I apparently needed even more tools I couldn't afford, large bunches of that excelsior stuff that was *not* lying around in my basement, plus some glass eyes imported at hideous expense from the Black Forest in Germany. Even if I came up with enough skill and patience to do the deed, which I now knew was a preposterous hope, I could never afford to mount a possum.

So I made my possum into a rug.

You've seen bearskin rugs. The sprawled-out skin is attached to a felt backing. The mouth is open and snarling to display all those fierce teeth. Well, that's just how I did my possum.

It seemed the neatest solution to a number of problems: The project would involve no body building, no excelsior, no fussy skinning, and no need for precise stitching. All I had to do was get the body off the skin, fill in the skull with a little clay to replace missing muscle tissue, stick in some eyes, and then somehow attach the possum to its felt backing (I figured glue would work). At long last, I had factors in my favor on this project. My father worked for a stuffed toy factory and had access to plastic eyes and felt, so I wouldn't have to buy them. And my little sister had some clay.

But I still lacked a couple of supplies. In order to preserve the skin and make it supple, I apparently needed some exotic tanning chemical. The School was willing—yea, even eager—to sell me the chemical, but the smallest can was distressingly large and expensive. I couldn't see buying enough KromeTone tanning salts to make an entire polar bear hide supple when all I wanted was to keep a fourteen-inch possum from rotting. Ah, but I'd learned there *is* a cheap and easy way to prevent flesh from decomposing: pickle it in alcohol.

Cheap and easy was always my way.

This time I saw the project through to the bitter end. The result, while not beautiful in the conventional sense, was extremely impressive. The eyes my father smuggled home were intended for a sizable teddy bear and weren't as strictly "naturalistic" as the glass eyes imported from the Black Forest. But in the head of my little possum, those jumbo plastic orbs had a stunning, pop-eyed effect. Possums start off with faces that could be a whole lot prettier, and when you give them eyes the size of a St. Bernard's, their expressions get downright intense.

I had not anticipated the fact that my "rug" would not be supple if it was pickled in alcohol. And it sure was not. Stiff as a board is what it was. Because I didn't know how to attach the skin to the skull, the lips of the possum began to curl and flare away from the mouth. By the time they stiffened, the possum was baring its fangs in a way that surpassed the shock value of any mounted grizzly bear you ever saw.

It wasn't much of a rug, either. If you were careful you could fit one bare foot on it, but nobody ever did that willingly.

The possum rug was the high-water mark of my taxidermy career. It was on display in my room until I was shipped off to camp one summer and my mother seized the chance to throw out a whole lot of stuff she was sorry I kept there.

Somehow, I knew better than to send a picture of my possum rug to J.J. Elwood (whose letters were now so testy I could no longer bring myself to open them).

Life goes on but, frankly, I was haunted by a sense of guilt about the whole episode. To this day, I can't hear the name "Omaha" without breaking out in a cold sweat. Not until many years later did I suspect that "J.J. Elwood" was probably a bored secretary who sat at a table all day, chain-smoking Kools and stuffing form letters in envelopes to keep youngsters climbing the twelve steps to SUCCESS and buying KromeTone tanning salts. The real J.J., to judge by the brochure photos, probably died long before I was born.

Do you suppose they stuffed him? Ha! Of *course* they did! I just wonder how they hid the stitches.

To Hell with Night Fishing

Night fishing for trout is just like war. That is, it consists of lengthy stretches of boredom punctuated by moments of stark terror.

Please understand: I am no less brave than most men. Courage is not the issue. It's just that some of us are more artistic and sensitive than average guys. We have more fully developed senses of imagination. Some of us see all the spooky things that lurk in ambush around dark rivers *plus* all those horrible things that *might* be there. Some men were simply never intended to bumble around in inky darkness on trout rivers in wild country.

Of course, most anglers never would consider doing such a thing anyway. Fly fishing in the dark is no easier than, say, playing tennis on a moonless night without court lights. Fly casting a brushy stream is hard enough when you can see all the branches you've wrapped your leader around, so casting in the dark inevitably results in a great deal of lost tackle. Doing anything at night on a midwestern trout stream is torture, for at sundown vampire hordes of mosquitoes patrol the rivers. Exsanguination is a slow form of death, I've heard.

There is only one reason for fishing at night: big trout. Daytime fishing—in the Midwest, at least—is fine for anglers content to catch trout that can be picked up with one hand if not, indeed, simply boosted out of the water by the leader. But if you want a taxidermy fish, you've got to be on the water when the old browns are active—the spooky old meat-eaters with lantern jaws and ruby spots the size of quarters. And that means you fish at night. In the dark.

And, really, there is nothing skulking around the average midwestern trout stream that is likely to kill a grown trout fisherman. Where I fish, you might run into snapping turtles, skunks, and porcupines, but they're just nuisances. Nothing . . . you know, life-threatening. Coyotes make ghoulish noises but keep their distance and mostly add atmosphere. The owls booming lugubriously from dead trees only *sound* like they'd fancy adding human flesh to their diet. And bears fear trout anglers more than we fear them. (If you can believe *that!*)

Yet, when I'm on a river at night and I can't see as far as my rod tip and I haven't heard a human voice for five hours, somehow my mind keeps drifting toward thoughts of crocodiles in the water, venomous snakes on the paths, vast sucking black holes in the bottom of the stream, and . . . well, just all those "Things" a guy can't see but damn well knows are out there. I'm an artist. I have a healthy, even hyperactive, sense of imagination.

I can make this clear through example.

One night, while fishing in the dark, I was sneaking up a moonlit little river when I met a beaver. I must have scared the beaver. I *know* he scared me, doing that business with his tail that beavers do so well. One moment I was slinking along with visions of giant trout; the next moment the river right beside my knee erupted in a violent explosion like someone had dropped a grenade in the stream. I nearly leapt clean free of my waders.

But I was back the very next night, hunting big trout. That was the night some waterlogged snag drifted downstream and swept up against my thighs. Or I should say a snag is what it turned out to be when I finally got the chance to examine it in the wavering beam of my Flex Light. All I knew at the time was that I suddenly felt something heavy in the water thumping insistently against my legs. "*Crocs! Crocs!*" I thought. Or maybe the drifting corpse of another night fisherman.

I tried to jump free as I had from the beaver. But this object had a more complicated shape, so I got tangled up in it when I came back down. Long before I comprehended that I was wrestling with an inanimate object, I totally lost my concentration on trophy trout.

Although I have been terrified on six different trout rivers (the only six I've fished at night), my moments of special horror have taken place on northwestern Wisconsin's White River. The White is a cold, wild, and enigmatic river. By day, you can study its reflective surface without getting the least hint that it holds trout.

At night, however, old cannibal browns slide out from the undercut banks and begin cruising the river. Then life isn't safe on the surface of the river for anything smaller than a beagle. When they suck a fly off the surface, these leviathan browns make the sound of a bratty kid honking hard on his straw as he bottoms out a chocolate malt. A friend once hooked a big White River brown. The fish towed his canoe up and down the river for several minutes before breaking off. Fish like that pick their teeth with trout of the size I usually catch. Like many other fish-eating carnivores, these old browns have halitosis that would gag a vulture.

That's the *good* news about night fishing the White. There is bad news. Nowhere on earth are mosquitoes thicker or more blood-thirsty than on the White. It's the only place where I have been driven to wearing a mesh headnet and *Playtex Living Gloves* while fishing. The White is the only place where I have felt the need to give my forward cast a bit of extra punch to force the line through packed swarms of insects.

And then there are the sinkholes. They're called "quicksand" by the local folk, but that's an exaggeration. You know how locals will talk. Sinkholes are just places where underground springs enter the sandy bottom of the White. They don't really suck you down. But that's small consolation when it's as dark as the inside of a cow and you step into a bottomless chamber of bubbling sand and water.

And then there are the surroundings. Where I fish the White, it winds through something called the Bibon Swamp. For some mysterious reason, all the streamside trees there are large and dead, their naked limbs reaching like snakes toward the night sky. Just one road crosses the river in seventeen miles. From the river you never see a farmhouse, a car, or any other artifact of civilization. You don't see any anglers out there, either; it's just you and the owls and the coyotes and the bears. Anyone who has seen Disney's depiction of Ichabod Crane's lonely night ride knows *exactly* what it's like to fish the White at night. I often think of old Ichabod when I'm night fishing. I identify with him. He was artistic, too.

Against my better judgment, and in spite of my advanced powers of imagination, for three years I frequently fished the White. Always at night. Usually alone.

In that time, I only met one sinkhole, but it was enough to give me the general idea. I was rushing upstream to get to a trout I could hear murdering May flies. I stepped out boldly with my right foot, only to find that the stream simply had no bottom where I'd put it. I went down, shipped water into my waders, and fled the stream, gargling curses through a mouthful of river water. By daylight, I learned that this particular sinkhole was barely large enough to admit a size nine boot. Just a baby as sinkholes go . . . but I was impressed.

And, oh, I should have learned! I should have known better than to fish the White in pitch blackness again. I should have realized I wasn't the kind of guy who should go banging around on a wild river with nothing but my vigorous imagination and a little moonlight to illuminate the surroundings. But I kept coming back for more.

Thus I was on the White one night during the famous *Hexagenia limbata* hatch. *Hexagenia* is the nation's largest May fly. The nymphs hatch in the dark, carpeting the river with their huge, meaty bodies. As you can imagine, the trout make pigs of themselves at such times, even cannibal browns that never otherwise lower themselves to the eating of bugs. The "Hex" hatch is the one chance for the dry fly angler to take a brown trout nearly as long as his arm.

My earlier fishing that night had only yielded several fish slightly longer than my hand. Then I heard one of the old assassins making that bottom-of-the-malt sound. His rises were so loud I could even hear them over the background drone of vampire mosquitoes. He was feeding around a bend in the river, so I edged around that bend to get in position for my cast.

Then, between one step and the next, the bottom of the river just wasn't there anymore. I thought I'd found my second sinkhole, but it turned out to be only a normal river hole with steeply sloping, sandy sides. I could hold my position on the slope if I kept backpedalling with my feet in the soft sand. It was touch-and-go, though. The river was lapping at the tops of my waders.

Okay, Mr. Cannibal Brown Trout, where are you? You have a date with a taxidermist, fish-breath!

I flopped out a cast. It wasn't much of a cast, but casting is awkward when you're holding both arms straight above your torso to keep your wader tops half an inch above the river. There was just enough reflected moonlight on the water to let me see my fly riding coils of current right back at me.

Then some *Thing* flew out of the night and smacked into my rod. I didn't know what it was then; I don't know what it was today. It had wings . . . that's all I know for sure. Call it a UFO. Ricocheting off my rod, this Thing flew up into my face and spent several moments fluttering against my right temple with its wings, as if seeking a passage through my head. I won't try to tell you how long it was there, because (as Al Einstein has pointed out) time is relative, not absolute. Especially when some unknown animal is going *bip, bip, bip!* with its little wings all over your head. In "relative" terms, the Thing was on my face for a short lifetime.

I let out a little groan of heartfelt fear.

Then the Thing wasn't there.

I looked down just in time to see my fly bobbing right toward me, inches under my nose (which was pretty close to the river by now, given how deep I'd waded). Just then Mr. Cannibal Brown Trout rose at my fly with a great, beaverish splash that threw water all over my face. I whooped and threw my rod skyward in a ludicrous attempt to set the hook. But since forty feet of slack line was lying in serpentine loops between my rod and the fly, all that accomplished was to launch the fly line into the sky. And all that line eventually piled up like so much spaghetti on my head.

Of course, the trout was gone.

I grabbed a tree on the bank and hauled myself out of the water. There I sat on a log until I calmed down a little. I smoked two large cigars before I could manage walking again. Back to the car.

The river was trying to tell me I didn't belong there, I now see. But did I see it then? Alas, no.

On another night, dark and spooky, I spent two hours cowering under an alder bush on the banks of the White. There was some animal with very heavy feet just a few yards away. Each time it moved, it shook trees and made the earth along the river bank vibrate. "BEAR!" I thought. It had noisy breath. As for me, I scarcely breathed the whole time, as I was desperately trying not to exude body scent where a keen-nosed carnivore could detect me. I never made a cast that night and ended up crawling back to my car on all fours before diving inside, locking all the doors, and spinning my wheels as I left.

Weeks later, I recalled having seen some thin, feral cattle grazing on that section of the White.

All of this, in a sense, set the scene psychologically for my last White River night fishing experience. It was an unusually cold night in late June. The sickle-shaped moon cast a little cold light over the Bibon Swamp. Since the Hex hatch had been running pretty good, I went out. I was alone, as usual, armed against the night only with my fly fishing gear, a Flex Light, and a squeeze-bottle of Cutter Repellent.

I took up a position on a particularly long pool. In fact, I'll tell you right where it was: three pools downstream of the UFO Pool, four pools upstream of the Bear Pool, and one pool above the Sinkhole Pool. I got to know that stretch of the White pretty well.

And there I stood, waiting two hours for the first fish to rise. It never did. Sometimes the hatch simply doesn't develop, and this was such a night. I began to feel foolish, standing there in all my expensive trout gear with no fish in sight. I was like the lounge lizard who dons his snappiest party clothes and cuts a dashing figure in a fern bar for hours without drawing the attention of anybody except the bartender.

Obviously, this wasn't my night to score. I was just making an ass of myself. Time to go home.

To relieve the tedium and warm myself with a little exercise, I knotted a Muddler Minnow to my leader and whipped it around as I slogged back downstream to my car. I lit a cigar for comfort. I was making a backcast when, somewhere out over the river's surface, I felt something whack my Muddler as it sailed back toward me.

I knew what it was right away. Bats had been wheeling over the river all night, gorging themselves on the blood-filled mosquitoes that had been gorging themselves on me. I was calm. I didn't panic. I was just miffed that a myopic little flying rat had screwed up a good backcast.

Then I looked down. There, silhouetted in the shimmering light of the moon, was the bat . . . about a foot away . . . swimming directly toward my belly button. The bat was apparently stuck on my Muddler's hook and trapped in the surface film of the river. It was coming straight at me where I stood in waist-deep water. I wish I could find words to describe how hideous it looked as it flailed the water with its webby wings.

At such moments, a person doesn't rationally calculate the risks. Or, at least, an artistic sort of a guy—a fellow with advanced powers of imagination—doesn't coolly conclude that a teeny little bat could never inflict a lethal bite through the thick hide of chest waders.

My only thought was to retreat. I moaned in horror and began backstepping as fast as I could. To be more precise, I backstepped *faster* than I could, because my legs could not execute the escape my panicky brain was demanding. You've seen this in cartoons, when a frightened character's legs whir so fast they separate themselves from the torso. Some people criticize cartoons for playing fast and loose with the Laws of Physics, but I've learned that the cartoons have it right. Given enough fear—and I *had* enough, with some to spare— the torso can't keep together with the legs.

I fell backward into the river, landing so violently I drove my fly reel deep into the sand of the river bottom. When I came up, the cigar still clenched in my teeth was offering little comfort.

And I learned there are worse things than falling on your ass in icy water at night on a spooky river with a mad bat hooked on your fly and apparently seeking revenge by sinking its bloody little teeth into your pink flesh. What is worse is coming back up again *not knowing where the bat might be* . . . like maybe on your soggy hat or *down* the neck of your soggy shirt or (*No, dear God, NO!*) DOWN THE FRONT OF YOUR WADERS!

Even then my cognitive powers did not fail me. In a flash, I knew what I had to do. I had to distance myself from the bat by getting up-current from it. I resumed my frantic backward scramble. And it was then that I spoke. As I recall, my words were: "*Aaa-haa! Whoooooooeeeeee! Sheeeeminy! Waugh! Waugh! Waugh!*

Garrrrrrgh!" I continued backpedalling at maximum speed, howling like a banshee until I was hoarse.

I don't know how far I travelled, but I had gone a considerable distance before I realized that the bat was no longer with me. Maybe seventy yards. I guess it doesn't matter. I finally perceived that I was all alone again, a full-grown man running backward up a trout river, drenched to his drawers, baying in terror at the moon.

I wound the fly line around the base of my sand-jammed reel and sloshed back toward my car and civilization. An owl in a tall dead tree demanded to know "*Who cooks for YOU?*" My rude reply (which sort of rhymed) need not be included here.

It seemed like a long drive home. Water gurgled musically around in my waders, which I hadn't removed. And I had time to reflect on my career as a night fisherman. Clearly, I was not ready for the sport. Clearly, I should confine my fishing to daylight hours until I was a little more mature, just a bit more self-confident. Some day I would be grown up enough to resume my pursuit of cannibal browns on dark, wild rivers, but not now.

That was nineteen years ago. I haven't felt ready yet.

Brinka's Hunting Education

For an embarrassingly long time—several years, in fact—Kathe and I hunted with a young Labrador who had a bizarre definition of "hunting." Brinka adored hunting, but she understood it about as well as she understood quantum physics.

Brinka wasn't stupid, nor did she lack desire. Quite the contrary. When retrieving a dummy thrown into a lake, Brinka was so eager to reach it that she moaned and gibbered nonstop while pumping the water with feet, tail, and ears for more speed. Brinka had more enthusiasm for hunting than you'd find in four average dogs. And she was both clever and biddable, which should have made her training a breeze.

In other words, Brinka should have been a great hunting dog and later became one when she finally caught on. She hunted so badly for so long simply because she did not get the proper schooling. In fact, her hunting education absolutely went off the rails, which is what this story is about. Consider it a case study in how not to train a dog.

There were reasons that things went so badly. There are always reasons, right? When Kathe and I got Brinka, I already had a hunting dog that was at least three times as much dog as I could handle. So I had no time for training Brinka. (And no qualifications, you would rush to add, if you had seen how well Brandy behaved.)

Anyway, Brinka was Kathe's dog and Kathe's responsibility to train. She planned to have Brinka hunt-ready for the 1977 season, but Kathe became preoccupied that summer because . . . well, *pregnant* is what she became, increasingly so as summer wound toward fall. She was too involved incubating to do much educating. Since Kathe was disinclined to lumber through the weeds to teach her pup how to hunt, Brinka's hunting education was put off.

Kathe did find time for yard training with Brinka. That was a pretty fair introduction to field work, actually, given the height of the weeds in my yard. Brinka learned *Sit*, *Stay*, *Come* and *Heel*.

She made blind retrieves from the thick stuff on the back side of the bird bath. Brinka even learned the command *Hide-your-eyes-so-the-ducks-don't-see-you!* (Brinka lies as low as a snake while holding paws over her eyes.) Kathe didn't hunt ducks, but if she ever started, she wasn't going to flare them with shiny Labrador eyes.

Kathe and I were cunning enough to time matters so the birth would take place in early September, after the best fishing and before bird season. But woodcock season came, followed two weeks later by grouse season, and Kathe was still pregnant . . . in fact, more pregnant than ever. This was the first time I tried to get my daughter to hold to a schedule, and it was a portent.

But pregnancies, even this one, are not permanent; they just seem so. Eventually Molly made her appearance. Three weeks later, Kathe felt strong enough to go grouse hunting. After all, Brinka was physically all grown up but still hadn't experienced her first hunt. We drove north with some friends, a young baby-sitter, baby Molly, and two enthusiastic dogs.

You know what grouse hunts are like. You've read your Burton Spiller, your George Bird Evans, your Michael McIntosh, William Harnden Foster, Joel Vance, Tom Huggler, and Steve Smith. Maybe even—God help us—your Steve Grooms. You already know grouse hunts are mellow, spiritually uplifting sojourns featuring great dog work, the king of upland birds, and spectacular surroundings during the loveliest time of year.

Well, forget every word you've read. This trip was as mellow as an IRS audit, as lovely as a goiter, and as spiritually uplifting as a proctoscopy.

In case you want it, I have the formula for a grouse trip from Hell.

Start with a newborn who disapproves of a mother who would desert her infant daughter to go kill birds. Molly didn't use those words exactly, but she made her point eloquently enough with howling that rivaled a civil defense siren. We didn't sleep much. Nobody in the resort slept much.

Now add some bitter weather and gunmetal-gray skies. Stir well, then mix in some wind and a slashing rain. That pretty much takes care of the lovely autumn foliage. Then subtract grouse from the general mix, for this was a grim year of low-cycle grouse scarcity. Simmer all this for a while in a big cauldron.

Then, just to spice things up, throw in one ticked-off porcupine—which must have been a nearly-nude porky when he was done being ticked-off, because he left most of his quills in Brandy's face, including ample numbers in the sensitive tissue of her nose, gums, and tongue. A friend and I pulled quills for an hour before concluding that Brandy had been so thoroughly porkied that she needed to be whisked to a vet's office and anesthetized to get out all the quills.

So now you've got a braying baby, foul weather, bad hunting, and a dog whose face resembles a pincushion—and who desperately needs medical attention.

Not a pretty picture, is it? It all adds up to a fairly disappointing grouse hunt. William Harnden Foster left out a few things when he eulogized the sport. But I have yet to mention the bad part of the trip. The *car* was the bad part.

Shortly after arriving at our grouse hunting grounds up north, I decided to take a quickie hunt to check out bird numbers. So I drove down a little two-rut logging road I'd never seen before. The "road" kept getting fainter and thinner. We drove about 14 miles deep into the empty heart of a state forest without seeing a living thing.

Suddenly our Volvo let out a tinny bleat and slammed to a halt as if it had hit a wall. It wouldn't go forward, and it certainly wouldn't go backward.

I know a thing or two about automobiles, so I examined the car. I became suspicious when I noticed that the right front wheel pointed southeast while the left pointed southwest. It seemed to me that wheels usually point more or less the same direction. We obviously were not going to drive out of the woods until the wheels agreed to work together again.

Kathe put Molly in a baby backpack and all six of us—two stressed-out adults, one shook-up baby-sitter, one bawling infant, and two grinning dogs—began hiking out along our backtrack. We were encouraged by the fact that the nearest human being couldn't be much more than seventeen miles away.

Imagine our astonishment and relief, then, when we saw a jeep bouncing through the middle of the woods. Its occupants, improbably enough, were two Indians. They turned out to be Ojibway tribal foresters, and they generously agreed to crawl under the Volvo. They mended my busted tie rod with baling wire and twine. Then they told me I should keep my speed down to 35 miles an hour and avoid turning the steering wheel.

Because the nearest Volvo parts were a week away (*if* we paid an outrageously expensive courier to bring them to the resort), we were obliged to drive the car in its jury-rigged condition for three days. Three days of trying to avoid left and right turns. Try it sometime. We even had to make the 280-mile return trip in heavy traffic at highway speeds, trusting baling wire and the power of prayer to keep the wheels rolling in the same direction. Try *that* sometime.

But that's a digression. We're talking about Brinka's hunting education here. The one positive outcome of the nightmarish trip was that we introduced Brinka to game.

On the first day of hunting (not counting our aborted scouting trip), I took Brinka out to show her a grouse. Like I said, hunting was slow. When I finally managed to knock a bird down, Brinka was excited. I gave her hand signals to send her in for the bird. She understood that I meant for her to do a retrieve. Yipping maniacally, she covered 25 yards in five great kangaroo bounces.

Suddenly Brinka's body seemed to shrink to half-size. Her tail clamped up to her tummy, her ears stuck out sideways, and the whites of her eyes showed big enough to flare a tame duck in a city park pond. Brinka looked at me as if to say, *"Sheesh Boss, there's a DEAD ANIMAL out here!"* I hollered and hopped about in futility before realizing that Brinka wouldn't touch the feathered corpse under any circumstances. I retrieved it myself.

This wasn't going well.

Then I had a brainstorm. I tossed the bird into the woods. Brinka would retrieve any thrown object, I knew, so maybe this little stunt would prime the pump and get her going. After six throws, Brinka overcame her disgust for the deceased grouse and began bringing it back to me. Soon she was so proud that she didn't want to let go of the bird, which, by now, was somewhat the worse for wear.

One small step for dogkind, but one big leap forward in Brinka's hunting education.

Then another grouse flushed, and I managed to clip it with the fringe of my pattern. The bird fluttered down in an alder swale, where I could not find it. Suddenly Brinka broke into a chorus of frenzied barks. I found her confronting the grouse, which she had backed up against an aspen stump. I dispatched the bird with mixed emotions. I'd never have found it without Brinka, but I wished she had retrieved it instead of *treed* it. It was exemplary work . . . for a coon hound.

I threw the dead bird a few times anyway. Brinka fetched it back the first time, holding a wing delicately in her teeth so her gums wouldn't touch the dead flesh. After several more throws, though, she was retrieving with a high head and whipping tail. I was proud of what we'd accomplished.

Kathe got to see her hunting pal in action the next day. She and Brinka were strolling together along a tote road when a young grouse made the mistake of flushing right down the trail. Kathe dumped it. "Something real odd happened then," she later told me. "I was putting the bird in my game bag when Brinka went *nuts*. She barked and cursed me and wouldn't calm down until I threw the bird a few times for her."

Brinka was beginning to get a fix on the mystery of "hunting." Parts of it were fuzzy, but at least she knew that Steve or Kathe would shoot something and then throw it five or six times so she could retrieve it.

I hunted with Brinka a few more times that fall. Kathe had her hands full with Molly, and Brinka still had a lot to learn. Brinka tagged along at my heels (*"Why risk getting lost in the woods?"*) and waited for Brandy to flush something so I could shoot it and then throw it for her. When the action got slow, Brinka would grab a stick or a corn stalk and implore me to throw it. Birds were fun, but she didn't see why we wasted so many chances to have her retrieve more available objects.

And that was where things stood after her first hunting season.

The next fall found Brinka still wildly enthusiastic about hunting . . . in her own way. It still didn't occur to her that finding birds or making them fly was her responsibility. Nor did she see why she should fetch them until I or Brandy had fetched and then thrown them for her.

Kathe wasn't altogether disappointed. She had spent too many years fighting the brush while watching Brandy bombing through the cover at enormous distances, flushing birds so far out of range that we could neither hear nor see them well. Having a dog that stuck close was nice, Kathe found. And you couldn't have asked for a more cheerful hunting companion than Brinka.

I was the one with problems. I was embarrassed to go about with a Labrador that stepped on my heels instead of quartering ahead to work birds up. I dreaded running into someone in the field who would recognize me, the outdoor writer. "Hey, Grooms! How come yer dog's *behind* you? Is this some advanced trick you haven't told us about yet? Har, har, har!" I kept trying to show Brinka that there was more to the hunting game than she'd grasped.

That's what we were doing one memorable day in October in a grouse covert in north-central Minnesota. Brinka and I were bumbling along together, she carrying a big stick (hoping I'd take notice and throw it) while Brandy ripped around us like a model airplane on a wire. Brandy doesn't miss much, so I was surprised when I almost stepped on a woodcock. It rose inches from my left boot and fluttered woozily off to the north like an inebriated butterfly.

My first shot, fired in total confusion, was nowhere near the disappearing 'cock. I shoved the gun ahead and yanked the trigger again. At the shot, the world seemed to explode in front of me. I had centered a teen-aged aspen that was only an inch or two from my muzzle. There was a tremendous shower of pulpy white splinters that obscured my view of the bird. The upper part of the tree began to wobble and reel, then toppled to earth. Incredibly, out of the corner of my eye, I thought I saw the woodcock go down, too.

Folks, I wish you could have been there. It was a proud moment. Brinka stood transfixed while she tried to process what she had just seen. She spat out her stick and stared some more. Then she executed one of the prettiest bits of dog work you'll ever see from a highly trained retriever: a *double retrieve*. It would have garnered more points in a trial if she had retrieved the more distant object—the woodcock—first, but she brought me the tree before fetching the bird.

Through the remainder of that season, Brinka carried herself with more assurance and pride. Yet I thought I detected a bit of confusion in her eyes when we passed saplings.

She seemed to be thinking: *Why doesn't Steve shoot trees more often, now that he's proved he can hit them?*

The Most Important Fish

Molly's bobber lies flat on its side, stuck in the surface film of the lake precisely where the airy world of humans meets the watery world of fish. My daughter and I are fishing from the shores of a city park. Molly is only three years old, so the junior-sized cooler we brought to keep our pop chilly doubles nicely as a seat for her.

A few yards away, a robin is engaged in tug-o-war with a surprisingly rubbery nightcrawler. The carpet of dandelions around us suggests that the Park Board is exercising chemical restraint this close to the lake. After the long winter, spring is going full tilt, and we can smell the thrust of surging life in the soil, grass, and lake.

"Look, Steve! What's that in the water?"

A painted turtle has popped to the surface close to Molly's bobber. It peers about owlishly before lowering periscope and paddling awkwardly toward the bottom. I've never understood what Mother Nature had in mind when she designed turtles. They are clumsy in the water and clumsier on land. Turtles don't seem engineered to do anything well except loaf in the sun. They're solar panels with tiny heads and feet.

"That's a turtle. He's called a painted turtle because his shell is so colorful. Underneath, where you can't see it."

"What's the turtle doing?"

"Probably looking for food, Molliwog. Or maybe just enjoying this nice day like we are. Turtles like to be warm."

"But what does he eat?"

What *do* turtles eat? Snappers eat fish, ducklings, and carrion, but I've never seen a painted turtle eat anything. Are they quick enough to catch insects? I'm stumped.

"I don't know, Muppet. When we get home we'll look it up in your big animal book."

Molly has many animal books. She has been fascinated by animals for as long as she has been aware of a world beyond her own skin. Of course, Kathe and I encourage this. We'll buy her any animal book that offers something new. By her third birthday, Molly could properly distinguish between the three big spotted cats: the leopard, jaguar, and cheetah. At her age I would have called them all "tigers."

Molly's bobber, all this while, has been stretched out lazily on the water, as lifeless as an old rug.

"Why don't I catch a fish? I want to catch a fish."

Molly is learning an unwelcome truth about fishing. She came along with me on this fresh May afternoon thinking that fishing was something like reaching into a jar to fetch out a jawbreaker. Now it dawns on her that fishing is a cooperative activity. That is, if the fish do not cooperate, she does not catch them.

"Be patient, Molliwog. I bet there's a fish staring at your worm right now."

Molly applies herself to the task of being patient. It isn't her strong suit. But when fish play hard-to-get, it isn't only kids who get antsy. One of the longest fishing trips of my life was the three hours I spent in a canoe with a high-powered executive from a toilet paper company. Every time a whole ten minutes passed without his getting a bite, he insisted I haul up the bow and stern anchors and move the canoe. Worse, when I caught a walleye, he wanted to swap places in the canoe so he could be closer to the honey hole. Molly, some fifty years younger than that fellow, is showing more maturity. But I'm beginning to get concerned. Molly may decide fishing is boring if her bobber doesn't move soon.

I haven't told her yet about the cookies in the baggie inside the cooler. They are my ace in the hole. No child dislikes any activity that includes cookies.

Why is it important to me that Molly learns to like fishing?

The question isn't easily answered. For starters, I have to admit to some purely selfish motives. Since I fish so much, it would be convenient for me if my whole family wanted to come along with me.

But there's more. Fishing is fun. All of it—futzing with tackle, teasing a weedless frog across a canopy of lily pads, the lyrical rhythm of fly casting, the cat-and-mouse strategizing, the splashy savagery of a surface strike—all of it is fun in ways that nothing else can be.

Then, too, fishing has taken me to places, wonderful places, that I would never have seen without the excuse of fishing to motivate me to go there. There was that dawn on the Brule when fog boiled off the river in twisty fingers. A young whitetail, his forked antlers cloaked in fuzzy velvet, stepped into the river ahead of us. He turned and began walking downstream with a ballerina's grace, passing just feet from our rod tips as we stood there afraid to breathe.

Fishing has been a wellspring of delights for me. I want Molly to share that pleasure.

Molly squirms on her little ice chest and stares disapprovingly at her bobber.

I find myself thinking back to the most important fish of my life. I didn't catch it; Kathe did. The fish made its appearance, spectacularly and unexpectedly, on a lazy summer afternoon when Kathe and I were newlyweds. We were wading the St. Croix River so I could try out the new fly rod I'd bought by selling my twelve-string guitar. When Kathe asked to try the rod, I was reluctant. Fly rods can be terribly frustrating when waved by inexperienced hands, and I didn't want her to be discouraged. Kathe's first cast dropped her bucktail streamer near some boulders close to shore.

There was a vicious boil. Then a three-pound smallmouth blasted through the surface film like a brick thrown through a mirror. The bass bulldogged a moment or two, then ricocheted across the top of the river like a skipping rock. Kathe let out a whoop, then dissolved in laughter while the smallie tried to fly and I bellowed conflicting instructions. I've often thanked that splendid bass. It gave me a lifelong fishing partner.

"See the bird over there, Molly?"

"Yup."

"What is it?"

"Duck."

"What kind of duck?"

"Mallard."

"Boy mallard or girl mallard?"

"Ummmm, boy. Girl mallards are brown."

"Good girl!"

I remember when Kathe began to fish. She began to look at water with a more specific and sophisticated interest than before. She taught me things about fishing I hadn't understood. Once she might have described a northwoods river as "pretty," but as an angler she'd notice whether crayfish were present, how fast the current was, and where the push of moving water was blunted by obstacles that would make good predator ambush points. Through trout fishing she learned the life cycles of caddis flies, stone flies, and May flies. Great Lakes fishing taught her the impact of water temperature on cold-blooded creatures. As all fishermen must, she became aware of weather.

All this, and so much more, is important and rewarding to study. I suppose we should educate ourselves about these things for their own sake, without the spur of catching fish to motivate us. Yet it doesn't work that way.

I have also come to respect the way fishing imposes discipline on each angler's understanding of fish. A fisherman constantly makes judgments about where fish are and what they will do in response to various offerings. Unlike more passive observers of the natural world, the angler repeatedly learns how accurate his or her theories are. The fish bite or they do not. Which is to say, they either confirm or deny the angler's hypotheses. It's always healthy when theory confronts reality.

Molly recoils at the sight of a strange creature hovering overhead.

"Oooh, Daddy! What's that?"

"Don't worry, Molly. That's just a harmless old dragonfly."

"But why is he flying like that and not moving?"

"He's probably looking for a mosquito. Dragonflies eat mosquitoes."

"What eats dragonflies?"

"Bass do. And some birds, I guess."

Molly has already outgrown the Walt Disney picture of nature. She knows animals eat animals. She understands that the cute baby antelope does not always escape the charge of the lioness. She knows the lioness must occasionally be successful or her cute cubs will starve. Molly still tends to moralize—"Are dragonflies good?"—but we're working on that.

I think again about my desire to have Molly love fishing. It worries me sometimes. Molly should be perfectly free to decide for herself what recreations she prefers. I know that, and yet the possibility she will reject fishing concerns me.

Perhaps this is perfectly normal, just as it is normal for devoutly religious parents to hope their children will embrace their faith. For me, a close involvement with the natural world is spiritually nourishing in much the same way religion is for other people. Kathe and I find that our lives gain much of their pleasure and meaning from the hours we spend camping under a sky sprinkled with stars, plying a canoe through the slalom course of a twisty stream, or drifting delicate flies to the fairy rings of rising trout.

Such hours are lovely, enchanting, restorative. Water is the nearly universal solvent for dirty objects, and time on the water is the best solvent for cleansing one's self of the dirt and stress of modern life. We hope someday Molly will know this.

Of course.

So as it turns out, I have some complex and heartfelt reasons for hoping Molly learns to enjoy fishing. It isn't just fishing, the activity of catching fish, that I'm so eager to share, important though that is. I want her to enjoy a lifestyle that embraces the values of the natural world. We are all animals, after all, drawing our lives from the same soil, water, and air. If Molly learns to love fishing, she will appreciate the need for clean water and a wholesome environment for fish, animals, and people. I think she'll be a stronger and healthier person if she feels close to the natural world.

Molly stands up, announcing, "I want to go home."

At the same moment, her bobber disappears.

It doesn't wiggle or twitch; it just dives out of sight. I holler, "*Set the hook!*" This frightens Molly. She does not know how to set a hook and does not like her dad yelling at her.

But the special angel that looks out for young anglers has taken care of the matter, for the fish has hooked itself. Panicked, Molly forgets to turn her reel handle. She begins to walk backwards from the lake. The fish kicks and sprays jewels of water as Molly tows it to shore.

It isn't quite a three-pound smallmouth and it doesn't try to fly, but a ten-inch largemouth bass looks mighty big in a child's hands.

I think I am looking at the second most important fish of my life.

Boogie Up a Buck

Every deer hunter has a story about their first buck. This is mine.

The story comes from my third season of deer hunting. But first I should maybe say something about my first two seasons.

I came to deer hunting late in life and needed guidance. According to people who tried to teach the sport to me, those who hunt deer by kicking them up and blazing away at their disappearing tails are mental midgets with cheesy morals. The only proper and effective technique, they taught me, is to sit in a tree all day making a noise like an apple. They told me I should try to sit perfectly still, "like a rock."

And frankly, it helps to have the mental make-up of a rock if you mean to hunt that way. A rock has the patience to hold a position without checking its watch every three minutes. A rock can sit still for days, even, without exploding its bladder. Of course, no rock is dumb enough to drink nine cups of coffee before going "on stand." Rocks would be terrific stand hunters if they could just shoot better.

But if your IQ is higher than a rock's, stand hunting is like taking a dump without the benefit of reading material, only it takes all day to do and doesn't feel as good. Time slows down like chilled molasses.

Or at least that's what I found. In my first two years of stand hunting, I spent a total of nine days—nine agonizingly dull days—of sounding like an apple, moving like a rock, and seeing exactly zero bucks, zero does, and zero fawns. The most exciting event of my first two years of stand hunting was: The Day I Watched the Mouse Eat Grass. I haven't been so bored since my kindergarten teacher made me spend an afternoon in the cloak room for making goo-goo eyes at Susie Stoever.

A guy on stand resorts to little tricks to pass the time. I keep things lively by inventing little incentives for good behavior: *Well, Steve-o, if you sit here perfectly still, you get to chew another LifeSaver when your shadow finally touches that stump.* Wow! Whoopee! And

I don't even *like* LifeSavers!

My favorite deer stand pastime is "checkering" my palms. If you push your hand hard enough against the checkering on your stock—voila!—you get checkered palms. Here's the neat part: In a few minutes the checkering fades, and you can do it over again. And then (see how much fascinating variety there is to this?) you can try to count all the little diamonds before they disappear. Then, by checkering yourself with the other side of the stock, you can figure out if that side has the same number of little diamonds. You can easily do four or five hours on stand if you get heavy into hand checkering, so don't believe anyone who says stand hunting is *boring!*

I will confess, though, that on my first year of deer hunting I read three of Robert Parker's "Spenser" novels in my stand. You might claim I didn't see a deer because I was reading; it is my adamant position that I read because I wasn't seeing deer. A queer sort of reading it was: read a page, peer for deer; read a page, peer for deer.

I had another handicap that year, namely a roaring head cold. Sitting silently for hours and hours was torture because postnasal drip was teasing my lungs like a feather. In spite of heroic self-control, about once an hour my body would erupt: *Hyack, hark, brk, brk, brk, brk, wheeer, wheery, waugh-ptoooooie!* This would shock the antlers off any deer in the surrounding forty acres, and then I'd *know* I wouldn't see a deer for at least another hour. By the time things had calmed down enough to where I might begin to expect a deer, the feather niggling my poor lungs would be twitching again, ready to trigger the next explosion.

In short, my first two deer seasons weren't encouraging. After sighting in my new deer rifle, I never fired it. Hadn't even had the safety off. And where I hunted in my third deer season—just up the hill from Lake Superior and almost in sight of Canada—the DNR allows no does to be shot because any "excess" deer are harvested by timber wolves. Which is neat, but thanks to the wolves, the land I hunted that year was about the worst deer range in the state.

On top of that, my deer stand on my third opening morning was one from which no deer (let alone a buck) had ever been sighted. Every other stand used by the Paradise Ridge Deer Hunter's

Association had a name—the "Bloody Ridge Stand," the "Ten Pointer Stand," the "Buck Buster Stand." Not this one. Nothing had happened there. Ever.

So my expectations were . . . modest.

Even so, I got up about four hours earlier than I usually do, six hours earlier than what feels good. I encased my body in layers of insulation until I looked like the Michelin Man. Then I hiked up the trail in the dark to the stand with no name.

I even took the trouble of gobbing around some goo from a mysterious little bottle labeled "Sex Lure." The man at the store told me the goo was actually the pee of an amorous doe, if you can believe that. (Now, *there's* a job even worse than being an outdoor writer— waiting around in a deer pen with a little bottle until a lust-crazed doe begins to piss, so you can rush over to fill it up.) Let's just say I had my suspicions. Who knows *what* they put in those little bottles?

On my third opening day, as on the ones before, I soon got chilled right to the marrow of my bones. The temperature was close to zero, and a stiff breeze was doing a good job of cooling me off where I stood on my platform nine feet up a birch tree. I wore so much puffy clothing that my arms couldn't touch my sides, but it takes a lot of clothing to sustain heat when you move nothing but eyeballs for hours on end.

I spent two hours disciplining myself to sit as still as a rock, but I finally ran out of LifeSavers and had no more incentives to be good. By then, the icy fingers of hypothermia gripped my liver. My choice was simple: Move or die. I moved.

I began to step from leg to leg, to start some blood circulating. That felt better. I added a bobbing motion to the stepping. That felt even better. I got my arms into the act. Hmmm, that felt even better, but my rifle was cramping my style. I hung it by its sling on a nail in the tree. My steps got more animated. By this time a heat-less sun was up over the big lake, casting my shadow out where I could see it on the ground in front of me.

I began to dance around with more and more enthusiasm, amusing myself by watching the little "shadow man" boogeying all over the forest floor. Pretty soon I was doing some mighty fancy stepping up on my elevated platform, like a fat, flame-orange go-go girl in a cage above a rowdy bar.

Oooooweee, shake that thang! GET DOWN! Yo, shadow man, you knockin' me out!

I turned the radio in my head up real loud:

THERE she go, just a-walkin' DOWN the street!
Singin' DOO wah diddy, diddy DUM diddy do!
She lookin' so FINE and she feelin' so . . .

SNAP! went a twig behind me.

Ohhhhhhhhhhhhhhhh, shit!

Did you ever play "Freeze" as a child? You run around until somebody hollers "Freeze!" and you have to hold that position?

I froze. My arms were outstretched like a guy conducting an orchestra; my butt stuck lewdly out to one side. Slowly, I rolled my eyes back in their sockets until they hurt, trying to look behind me.

Omigod! It's a *deer!*

A deer. Just imagine that! A *deer!* The very last thing on earth I expected to see. A sasquatch wouldn't have surprised me more. They're spotted pretty often in wild places, you know. I figured I was pretty likely to see Nessie, being so close to Lake Superior and all. And Elvis . . . well, everyone sees Elvis sooner or later, although usually in K-Mart during a Blue Light Special.

But a *deer!* Frankly, it hadn't seriously occurred to me that a deer might walk up behind my no-name deer stand.

And I died inside. I thought, "This sucker's *got* me. Here I am, frozen in space like a blaze-orange Chubby Checker twistin' the night away. The deer is 20 yards away, staring daggers at me, and I've got a strong breeze blowing my rotten predator breath directly at it. No way I can shoot—I've got fat 'shearling' mittens on both hands. Worse, my rifle is hanging from a nail in the tree behind me. Or that's where I think it is, only I don't dare turn around to look. I am *SCREWN.*

"Oh well, I think it's a doe anyway. Can't shoot lady deer. Gotta be a doe. This is the first deer I've ever seen on stand. You always see 18 does and 48 fawns before you see something with horns. Everyone knows that. Gotta be a doe. I don't see any horns, although my eyes are kinda watery. Gotta be a doe."

I began to get ready anyway, just for practice. After all, this was the first deer ever to walk near one of my stands, and I wasn't about to waste the chance to practice with it. I crept my left hand toward the rifle while madly wiggling fingers to work off the right-hand mitten. "Be good, mitten! Be good. Come off like a nice little mitten. Atta baby! Now where is the pocket in this jacket?" (And I was going *stuff*, *stuff*, *stuff* with the mitten, trying to hit the pocket on this jacket I've only worn once before in my life.) "PLEASE don't fall *kerwhump* on the ground, mitten!"

By then I had something that felt like my rifle in my left hand; my right hand was naked. Of course, I was still facing the wrong direction and could only see the deer at the fringes of my blurry vision.

The deer stared at me, hard. I froze. It put its head down. I moved a little, trying to lift the rifle free of the nail without whanging the tree. With every tiny move I made, the rustling of my nylon parka was deafening. The deer snapped its head back up. I froze. It sniffed the wind suspiciously. Golly, what *was* in that little bottle?

And then I knew: "*JESUS, IT'S A BUCK! Oh, noooooooo! Itsabuck! Itsabuck!* I can shoot at it, if it doesn't bound away! Which it surely will. One hop, one crummy little bunny hop, and he's gone-zo! Acch! Be still, my heart, this ain't for practice anymore!"

I had been fine—well, reasonably calm and collected—as long as I "knew" this was a doe and "knew" it was going to dash away at any moment. At precisely the same moment when it dawned on me I could fire my first shot at a big animal . . . buck fever arrived.

Buck fever did not arrive in my whole body; it struck my right leg, which suddenly began whipping around like an egg beater. For a moment, I thought it was 1958 again and I was down in the basement lip-synching to Elvis records. I stared at the leg and willed it to be still. It went faster. The rest of me had stopped dancing, but my right leg was really getting it on.

I couldn't believe the deer would stand there directly downwind of the biggest, stinkiest blob of blaze orange it had ever seen. "What's wrong with this deer? Is it blind? Deef? Does it got no nose?"

My whirling leg made an aimed shot impossible from the offhand position, so I leaned into the tree to steady my upper body. Go ahead, leg. Express yourself. See if *I* care.

I began to level the rifle.

To my astonishment, the deer stood still while I moved the rifle, then turned broadside to present a profile like a plaster lawn ornament. It was the kind of pose the outdoor magazines say you'll *never* see in the woods. When my scope came up on him, his chest filled the 2X optic. I did not s-q-u-e-e-z-e off the shot, because I couldn't believe I had the luxury of taking that much time. Surely, the buck was going to rocket away from there any second now. When the crosshairs were high on his chest, *WHAM!*

At the shot, the deer turned and began to walk casually down the trail toward the lake. He looked perfectly healthy, maybe a little disappointed. I couldn't work the bolt fast enough for a second shot, so I stared in horror as he strolled out of sight. The voice in my head shrieked: "Don't *do* that, deer! I just killed you, didn't I?"

And then, nothing. Utter silence. Nothing looking back at me but the same old dumb shrubs and trees. It was spooky.

I hung my rifle on a step of the ladder and tried to scramble down. In the heat of the moment I forgot that tree stand ladders slant *in* toward the base of the tree. That's why I spent several agonizing seconds dangling by my fingers from the stand, legs churning in space, like a hanged man.

When I got to where the deer had been, there was nothing. No deer. No blood. No tracks. Nada.

What a strange feeling! I thought, "Jeeez, did any of this really happen? There *was* a deer here, wasn't there? I *did* shoot, didn't I? If there was a deer, did I totally miss a broadside buck at 20 paces with a scoped .270?"

Then I spotted a sprinkle of blood and a tiny tuft of hair. It was pink blood, lung blood, according to stuff I've read. I felt a flood of warm, blessed relief. It hadn't been a "dream" deer after all. I hadn't funked it.

The pink sprinkles led down the hill. Right to the last, the deer continued to be astonishingly cooperative. He walked 50 yards downhill before piling up on the main trail. If I'd hit him a bit further back, he would have made it all the way to my car.

The Paradise Ridge Deer Hunters Association traditionally meets at the "Top Of The Meadow" at midday to share stories and eat lunch. When we met that noon, I was full of helpful advice and observations on deer hunting. You know, friendly little tips from a Successful Hunter. I had a lot to say about the most effective ways to use Sex Lure. I took a certain amount of modest pride in my clean, one-shot kill (although my buck was killed at a distance where most hunters couldn't have missed with a spear). I even demonstrated the dance steps I'd been using.

Well, you know how it is.

Everybody has a story about their first buck, and I finally had mine.

Of Wilderness Steelhead and Pulp Mill Strippers

This is the tale of a steelhead trip taken one April several years ago. The story is true in all respects, though some names have been changed to protect certain innocent persons and places (as well as some that are foul, wicked, and utterly debauched).

Four men went on this trip—two steelhead experts and two novices. Though our original idea was to catch fish, you should know that steelhead ultimately had very little to do with the events of the trip. In fact, you might want to exercise precautions about whom you allow to read this story, for it might confirm the darkest suspicions wives have long harbored about what their spouses' "fishing trips" are really like.

These were the novices: Charlie had caught one steelhead previously, if you call a thirteen-inch rainbow a steelhead; but when you've chased them as long and as futilely as Charlie has, you *do* call a thirteen-incher a steelhead. Charlie's finest day of steelheading was that sunny afternoon on Wisconsin's Brule River when he lost eight hooked fish. I didn't do so well, only managing to lose one that day. Which left my lifetime total at one steelhead accidentally snagged and released, plus one legally landed.

Like I said, novices.

These were the experts: At the time, Bill lived in steelhead country and had caught more than his share. Bill's only shortcoming as a steelheader is that he overprepares, for instance by carrying a lifetime supply of split shot in his fishing vest (plus four times that much in his kit back in camp). If Bill were to fall into a river he'd be no more capable of rising than a medieval knight in armor.

Doug, the other expert, could never be accused of overpreparing. While Bill worries about things that will probably never happen, Doug doesn't give a thought to the dreadful things that almost surely will happen. Doug and Bill nearly drowned in Lake Superior once when they ran far off shore in Doug's boat, which happened to have an eight-inch hole in its hull. Doug later admitted he'd felt there was "something funny" about the way the boat had been handling lately. Doug is an excellent steelheader, with the hands of a safecracker and the patience of a tree.

This was our plan: We would travel to a remote and lovely wilderness stream on the Canadian shore of Lake Superior. Bill first heard about the Crystal River in a bar frequented by North Shore steelheaders. According to hazy legends and hints whispered through beery breath, the Crystal is a virgin stream where a good man could take a dozen steelhead in a day. The Crystal River, Bill heard, is the pot of gold lying under the rainbow of every steelheader's dream.

But every pot of gold is protected by a dragon. The dragon guarding the Crystal is Lake Superior, the deadliest lake in America, the lake (it is said) that "ne'er gives up its dead." The Crystal flows through some of Ontario's wildest land, lying deep inside an undeveloped park. No permanent works of humankind are tolerated there, so no roads pass anywhere near the Crystal. If you wish to fish this enchanted river, you must take a boat ride. And unless you are very stupid, the boat ride will terrify you.

From the mouth of the Axe River where you launch, you make a run of several hours along a lonely shoreline before arriving at the Crystal. That shore is exposed to winds from three directions of the compass, the three directions most likely to kick out a wind in spring. So the boat ride will be lumpy more often than not, and frequently too hazardous to attempt. These waters have uncharted reefs and numerous waterlogged trees floating just below the waterline, where they are hard to see. And you really want to see them, because they are big enough to smash a propeller or punch a hole in a hull.

But if you manage to survive the boat ride, you can set up a tent camp at the mouth of the river. Then you enjoy the finest steelheading of your life.

So much for the plan.

This, as opposed to the plan, is what happened:

Bill, Charlie, and I traveled together, trailering my small boat to Kimberly, the closest town to the Axe River launch site. Working from an uninformative brochure, Bill had selected the McKinley

Hotel in downtown Kimberly as our meeting place. Remarkably, we all met at the McKinley on time.

That was not easy for Doug. He drives a 4WD PowerWagon that some kid customized as a Monster Truck. Doug's vehicle had been jacked up so high I could only get in it by taking a running start and making a perilous leap for the running board. Once I tried to enter by grabbing the door handle and clambering up with my feet, but that left me dangling upside down, unable either to enter the cab or let go of the handle. The radical reconfiguration of the truck's driveline causes it to go through axle components like a tree shredder chewing up Dutch elms. Doug spent a lot of time under his truck with vise grips, fixing sick U-joints. But he made it.

In my naivete, I'd pictured Kimberly as a quaint little fishing town, or perhaps a quaint little tourist trap, with stores selling coffee-can tom-toms, moose turds encased in plastic, and dolls dressed up as Mounties. I had not pictured it as a sullen mill town with blocks of sooty, ticky-tacky, cracker-box houses. The mill itself, wreathed in sinister plumes of steam (turned a sick pink color by the security lights), had a uniquely arrogant ugliness. By *mill* I mean *pulp mill*. The town's air was saturated with the smell of it, with not so much the stench of sewage as the stench of *old* sewage.

The McKinley turned out to be a shabby, three-story wood structure with most of its first story given over to an L-shaped barroom the size of a basketball stadium. This was not just a bar for friendly tippling but a grand arena meant to accommodate legions of grimly serious, two-fisted drinkers. The hotel's reception desk was locked and unoccupied when we arrived, so we ran down a barmaid and tried to register with her. "I can't talk now," she gulped, her eyes wide with fear. "They get *real* ugly if I don't keep coming around with beer."

She referred, obviously enough, to the patrons slumped around the tables in the barroom. They were about a hundred young Canadians dressed in toques, flannel shirts, and nylon jackets like the "Great White North's" Bob and Doug McKenzie. Some were stumbling drunk, the rest comatose. We finally got keys to Rooms 213 and 215. While waiting, we were surprised to be passed in the lobby by a nubile young woman wearing a lumberjack shirt and nothing else.

Room 213 was no surprise after what we'd already seen. Wallpaper sagged from the walls in patches. The linoleum floor had paths grooved in it. The beds were of the "deep valley" design, with mattresses contoured like the inside of a canoe. The windows were jammed shut, sealing in the fetid hotel air, so we spent some frantic minutes trying to pry them open. We finally propped one window up with a Gideon Bible and pieces of the desk, letting "fresh" pulp mill air waft in. That's when we learned that Canada's busiest railroad ran right behind the McKinley, almost close enough to touch.

Room 215, on the other hand, *was* a surprise—even after what we'd seen. When Charlie opened the door he was struck by an atmosphere heavy with the steam of a recent shower and the smell of cheap shaving lotion. A nude man sat on the bed, glowering at us but saying nothing. It was an awkward social situation. We had the key. He had the room. It was a Mexican standoff.

Charlie sought the manager (a surly, rotund fellow named Dennis, with a thin Brit mustache) to get an explanation and perhaps an apology for our inconvenience. Dennis offered neither, but instead launched into a sulfurous tirade. "That COCKSUCKER!" he shrieked. "Thinks he can waltz his fuckin' ass in here any ol' time, eh? Well, I'll ream *his* ass! He's not gonna fuckin' get away with this any fuckin' more!" With that, he threw the key for 320 at Charlie and stormed off to confront the fragrant cocksucker in 215.

Because the rooms had no televisions or radios, there wasn't a whole lot to do there, so we elected to patronize the bar before turning in. I became concerned about the safety of our boats in the hotel's parking lot. Out there I found a chubby man stumbling around in circles behind the boats. He kept muttering earnestly, "Theesh ish *nishe* motors!" I conversed with him for a while, turning constantly so nobody could sneak up behind me. When I determined he wasn't capable of unhooking the motors even if he spent the whole night trying, I rejoined our group.

The night was assuming an air of unreality. I leaned back in my chair and came eyeball-to-navel with a barefoot young woman dressed—to the extent she was dressed—like Pocahontas. She had a tough face and a hard, young body that needed no assistance from support garments.

The music suddenly changed. Pocahontas hopped on a little stage and began exchanging her Indian suit for her birthday suit. Few of the patrons—most of whom were face-down, blowing bubbles in the beery tabletops—seemed aware she was there. Between dancing sets, the "shaker" (as strippers are called in Ontario) sat at a table wearing a lumberjack shirt, legs demurely crossed, negotiating short dates with those customers sober enough to manage the flight of stairs up to her room.

Foolishly, we elected to take breakfast the next morning in the McKinley. When we ordered French toast and bacon for all hands, the waitress was outraged. "Why do youse do this to me?" she snapped in the dialect of a gangster. Thereafter she refused to say another word to us, serving the poorly prepared food in icy silence. We kept our tips modest.

We then consulted briefly with park officials. They told us the mouth of the Crystal might be iced up, which would prevent us from getting in to fish it. They thought we were two weeks too early to catch steelhead. The park manager's secretary, hearing we'd spent the night at the McKinley, blanched and looked ill. She emphatically recommended we move to a nearby motel that she described as a "family place."

Then to the Axe River. When we got to it, on Friday the 13th, the Axe was almost out of its banks due to a heavy melt of snow. The swollen river ran the color of putty. Surging in its violent currents were blocks of rotten ice as big as school buses, plus floating debris that included trees three stories tall. Somewhere upstream of us, winter was dying violently.

Just above the launch site, a logging company was dynamiting the river ice to clear the way for a huge log boom they were setting up. Just below it, the Ontario Provincial Police were dragging for the corpse of a fisherman who had drowned there nine days earlier. Two men had fallen overboard and died almost instantly in the numbing waters. One body had been recovered, but Lake Superior (it was said) refused to give up the other.

The scene was unsettling. We'd come seeking the bright beauty of wilderness steelhead. We'd found, instead, dynamite, death, and a river running like diarrhea.

Though the omens were bad, we made our first assault on Superior. We loaded the boats with gear until they nearly sank, then threaded our way downstream between logs and icebergs to test the waters of the big lake. Charlie had wanted to be in Doug's boat, the bigger boat, but reconsidered when he saw the gas cans. Doug had six gas cans under his feet, all leaking freely. And Doug is a chain-smoker.

It wasn't a good day for boating. A stiff breeze was whipping Superior into whitecaps. Giant haystacks mounted skyward where the force of the Axe met Superior's swells. Perilously little freeboard stood between us and the putty-colored death that swirled and heaved all around. We knew there would not be one soul to help us if we swamped, hit a reef, or impaled our boats on a log in all the miles of shoreline between us and the Crystal . . . which might or might not be ice-free and fishable if we even lived to see it.

I finally determined that we were insane to attempt the run in such conditions. I whipped the bow around and worked my way back to the launch site. A visibly peeved Doug wanted to go on, but I proudly told Charlie, "We know something now we didn't know half an hour ago: *We won't die here today.*"

Another steelhead stream lies near Kimberly. We re-trailered the boats and drove to the Black to get some fishing in before sunset. What we found there confirmed our fears about the condition of the Crystal. The banks were so deep with snow that walking them would have been possible only on snowshoes. The water was just a degree or two warmer than ice. But we fished it in spite of logic, for that is the essence of steelheading.

Miraculously enough, the two klutzes scored. Charlie's steelie was first, a truly unlucky fish that missed the hook but tangled his teeth in the bridal veil of the spawn bag. My fish came from the same hole, fighting as well as any semi-frozen fish can be expected to.

We celebrated our success that night with several bottles of

Canadian ale and with steaks we sizzled over a campfire kicking out cheery flames. A game warden dropped by. He was amazed we'd caught fish so early. He was even more amazed that we'd slept at the McKinley. "The *McKinley*, eh? Hey, that's a good one, eh? Nobody told you, eh?"

Full of the sweet taste of victory and a few Canadian beers, we climbed into Bill's warm truck for the trip to the "family place" motel. The last thing I heard before dozing off was Bill saying, "At least we'll get an early start tomorrow because we won't waste time tonight at the McKinley."

When I woke up, we were walking into the barroom of the McKinley. "Doug wanted to see the shaker again," Charlie explained.

The old gang was there. By their looks, beer sales had been brisk. As before, half of them sat bent over, blissfully asleep, while the others peered about with the glassy, confused expressions of owls caught in bright daylight. One stocky kid kept clambering onto the stage to perform his imitation of the shaker's bumps and grinds. He lacked her qualifications.

Then she appeared, this time in the guise of a leopard. She wore a little cat mask and a spotted suit with a long tail. During the first record of her four-record set, the shaker gyrated energetically around the stage on a pair of extremely high spiked-heel shoes. Meanwhile, the stocky kid shied coins at her from just offstage, egging her on.

Finally the first article of clothing came off—a belt. She twirled it in the air, holding the tag end while the massive brass fastener whistled around her head with a *whooo-wooo-wooo!* sound. It looked like part of the dance.

Her attack came with no warning. The shaker shot off the stage like a weasel going for a rabbit. She began to rearrange the face of the heckler, whipping him with that brass buckle. He was sitting in a chair and was unable to retreat, so he fell forward and wrapped his arms around the shaker. Their bodies teetered a moment, then went sprawling across a pool table.

There was a delay, during which the stunned audience struggled to comprehend what was happening. Then the crowd let out a collective howl and surged forward to rescue the kid (who, frankly, was way out of his league).

Order was finally restored. Two waitresses, holding an elbow each, led the shaker back onstage to finish her act. She was crying (*poor, misunderstood artiste!*), daubing tears and mascara from her eyes with the leopard tail.

The waitresses loosened their grip on her.

This enabled the shaker to launch her second attack. The crowd had confiscated her belt, so this time she worked the heckler's groin and face over with machine-gun bursts from her spiked heels. Again the crowd roared and threw itself upon the shaker and her victim, until the whole scene resembled a bench-clearing NHL brawl.

This time the waitresses pinned her arms with determination as they hauled her away. We finally understood that there would be no more dancing that night, so we retired to the family motel.

Then came The Day Of The Great Debate. The winds whooped all morning, lashing Superior into waves upon which I refused to go boating. Charlie and I burned to return to the Black, where *even we* could catch a steelhead and do it without becoming fodder for Superior's bottom-feeding fish. Doug and Bill hated to give up on the original objective, the Crystal.

The five-hour debate can be summed up neatly, as it repeated itself like a stuck record.

Doug: I think I could have made it yesterday in my boat.

Steve: I *know* I couldn't have made it in mine.

Doug: We could have made it if we'd had two boats like mine.

Charlie: Doug, we don't *have* two boats like yours.

Doug: Gee, I didn't come all the way across Canada just to turn around.

Steve: I didn't come all this way just to *die.*

Doug: I think I could have made it yesterday in my boat.

Steve: I *know* I couldn't have made it in mine.

At one point, Doug left briefly to seek a bathroom. Charlie and I pleaded with Bill to take our side. We made it clear how dearly we valued our lives. As fathers, husbands, and taxpayers, we felt an obligation to avoid drowning this early in our careers. Bill said, "If you feel that strongly, we obviously shouldn't go. That's alright. I can talk Doug into changing plans. I'm a very assertive person."

When Doug came back, the stuck-record conversation resumed. "Gee, we're so close, it's a shame to turn back," said Doug. Bill—good old assertive Bill—studied the toes of his boots for a minute while Charlie and I held our breath. Then Bill said, "Well, you know . . . we *are* pretty close."

During another recess in the debate, I had a chat with an Ontario policeman who had his own opinion of our plans. He had witnessed our first launch.

"I was surprised to see you guys go out there yesterday," he said, not smiling *at all*.

I told him we were being careful.

He said, "That really surprised me."

I repeated that we had been cautious.

He replied, "I've spent the last nine days dragging for that fisherman's body. I don't want to spend the next nine dragging for yours."

Touched by his concern for our well-being, I promised we'd wear vests so our bodies would float.

That afternoon we made our second assault on Superior. When we checked the lake's condition late that afternoon, the world's mightiest lake was tossing with icy malice. I was relieved.

Then the winds slacked and the lake laid down a little bit. It was time to *carpe* the *diem*. We launched, cracked the throttles, and roared away to the Crystal.

It was a wild trip. In my little boat, I had to negotiate each wave individually, gunning the motor and choosing the angle of attack before sledding down the back side, black water sucking at the transom. At one point I reflected that people pay good money at amusement parks to get half as scared as I was.

We ultimately arrived at the Crystal. The river had thawed just enough to let us slip in. It was as beautiful as we'd heard. I think the Good Lord was all set to rest after six days of making the world when he said, "Shoot, I'll make one more little steelhead river. And this time, *I'll get it just right!*" We set up camp, ate, and toasted the wilderness with Canadian beer.

Sadly enough, the next day and a half can be quickly summed up. We were two weeks early. The Crystal was snow lined and ice-cold. Under the circumstances, there were only two or three places a steelhead might hold. Bill and Doug, the good fishermen, found those places and jerked out a fish apiece. Charlie and I stamped up and down the snowy river muttering about how much fun we could have had on the Black. The novices never had a bump from a fish.

We still managed to enjoy ourselves. I spent an hour one afternoon hurling rocks at a very patient ruffed grouse. We took a side trip to another river, finding tracks and poo left by a caribou on a sand beach. I'd never seen caribou poo before. We drank the beer. At night we tipped back our lawn chairs on the beach to study the shockingly bright display of stars. On several evenings a male woodcock peented and performed death-defying power dives to attract a lady woodcock.

It was nice. Soon we had to return.

There was a final lunatic episode. Charlie and I had extracted a promise that we'd get to fish the Black on the way back. Charlie was in a fever to get back to the hole where he and I had taken our fish, a pool that lay just downstream from a little island. In his giddy haste, Charlie failed to notice that the river had risen two feet with meltwater since we'd fished it. A careful man with a wading staff would have known better than to attempt the crossing. Charlie, all his thoughts on steelhead, *ran* through the water without even looking while he strung up his rod and jabbered gaily to me over his shoulder.

Bill watched in horror as Charlie's mindless dash carried him to the island. Bill shouted, "Charlie, don't *consider* leaving that island until we're ready to help you!" We later returned with a long rope, which we threw across the snarling currents to Charlie. While Bill held the rope attached to Charlie's waist, I waited downstream to catch him if the river knocked him off his feet.

All that, as I mentioned before, took place a number of years ago. I've been back to Kimberly and the Crystal three times now. I was really afraid to try the trip again, but Bill wanted to go. And Bill is a very assertive guy. Believe it or not, we experienced several days when a good man could catch a dozen steelhead—even a few days when a mediocre man could do it.

I'm obliged to report that things in Kimberly are not the same. We were told that the shaker was run out of town after the night of the big fight. So we had witnessed her swan song, her last dance in that town. She was brought up on charges of prostitution and "assault with intent of bodily damage."

But I was there, and that's not what happened. She didn't intend bodily damage. She intended castration at the very least—and quite possibly homicide—but the law is not always precise about these things. Wherever she is now, I'm sure things aren't dull.

Nor is the McKinley the same. That old whore has been rehabilitated and gussied up; it's not even recognizable any more. A yuppie breakfast nook now stands where the shaker once shook those marvelous breasts. The diner features nostalgic photos from the days of lumbering and lacy gingham shades on the lamps. It's real cute now and slightly pricey. A "family place," you might say.

Gold made the difference. Kimberly is home to Canada's new gold rush. The town now reeks of money as well as *Eau de Pulp*. The ticky-tacky row houses wear fresh paint, and parked in front of each is a shiny pickup. Nobody in Kimberly is so poor that they have to drive last year's pickup.

And so another rowdy town has been brought to heel, another wild place tamed.

Perversely, I liked the place better when it still had hair on it.

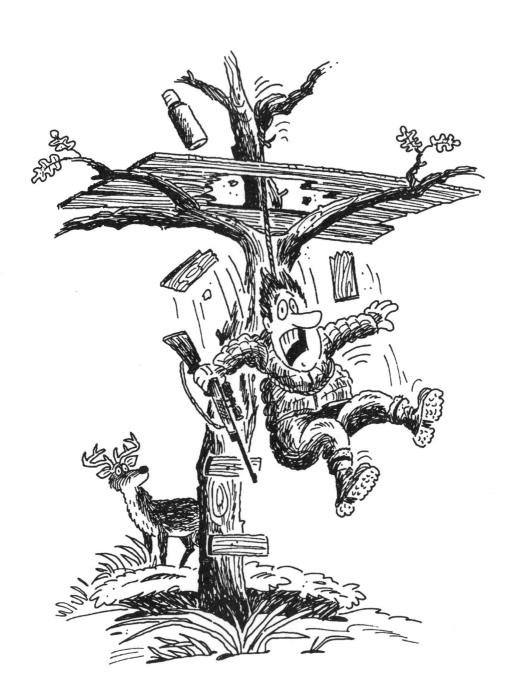

Fear and Trembling
on Deer Stand

It seems to be my special destiny to be the Clown Prince of deer hunting. Every year I sally forth in my blaze-orange clown suit with visions of posing, Proud Hunter, with my foot on the rut-swollen neck of a 12-pointer. Every year I encounter fear, boredom, and utter incompetence in a depressing variety of forms.

I did it again in 1988, the year I hunted deer in Wisconsin for the first time. I did not, as they say, "get my deer." Hell, I didn't even get anybody else's deer. I am psychologically ill-suited to "waiting" types of hunting, especially stand hunting for deer, which is basically a form of ambush.

Anyway, it's hard to perform admirably in an enterprise in which nothing happens—nothing, nothing, nothing—for hours on end, for *days* on end. And then suddenly you face the Moment of Truth as you stand there sucking a breath mint, fantasizing about Julia Roberts, and looking the wrong way. It's difficult to keep your mind focused on a blank landscape unless you have the mind of a Chia Pet.

As it happened, in my first Wisconsin deer hunt, I did at least see and shoot at a deer.

And I was ready for him, or as ready as I ever get. I had been mentally rehearsing this exact moment. I knew exactly what I should do if a deer were to show up.

Then, amazingly, here he came, a confused forkhorn capering down a hill of cutover aspen in plain sight. He was running straight into my ambush when he smelled my cigar breath and stopped to check out the scene, some 250 yards from me. Coolly, I snuggled down in the blind to get a rest for my rifle. With a deft motion, I dialed up the power of my variable scope so I could confirm the presence of his tiny antlers at that distance.

Just the way I'd rehearsed it.

But dialing the scope power up caused the field of view to zoom down—to almost nothing. I couldn't find his antlers to study them for legal length because I could not find the *deer* in my scope. I kept raising my head, spotting the deer, then trying again to find him in the scope. Over and over.

Steve to Scope: Scope, there's a damn deer out there!

Scope to Steve: Deer? What deer? I don't see no deer.

I had discovered what science fiction writers call the "parallel universe," and I was now hung up between two worlds. There was a buck out there in the real world, but he refused to materialize in the tiny world visible in my scope. I finally made a map of every little weed and shrub in that landscape, memorized their sequence, then systematically traced that sequence through the scope like connecting a dot-to-dot puzzle.

Aha! There you are, sucker! Say your prayers! You're history! You're venison!

By this time, however, my venison sensed he had become an actor in a play with a queer script. He set off walking, then accelerated. I am not a good enough shot to nail a moving deer at 250 yards, and I proved it. Very noisily. Four times.

At least I learned a few things about the sport. I learned, for example, that Wisconsin deer hunting differs from Minnesota deer hunting in several respects.

In Minnesota, you scout the cover to learn where the deer feed, where they sleep, and where they go to make whoopee. Then you build a big, comfy deer stand somewhere along the deer sidewalks that connect those areas.

In Wisconsin, you scout the locations of hunters, not deer. Each year you check out the locations of the guys from Baraboo, the gang that always stays at End O' the Trail, and the local boys who communicate with each other by honking their truck horns. Knowing where the people will be, you set up your ambush in places into which other hunters will stampede the deer. In this sense, a Wisconsin deer hunt is like a classic English country-manor pheasant shoot, with beaters driving the startled game toward the guns.

There is another remarkable difference between Wisconsin and Minnesota deer hunts. In Wisconsin it's illegal to erect the stable and commodious permanent deer stands I have known in Minnesota. Minnesota stands have bench seats and back rests and safety railings, plus they are big—real big. There are deer stands all over northern Minnesota with little plaques that say, "Steve Grooms slept here."

I suffer from vertigo, which is a polite way of saying I'm scared spitless by heights, any heights, like three feet off the ground. I can't climb a stepladder without pitons, safety ropes, and two burly body builders at the bottom to steady the damn thing. I once clambered up on my roof to re-aim my television antenna. My house, I should explain, has one story and a nearly flat roof. Nevertheless, I got trapped up there, paralyzed by fear like a house cat up a tree. With my arms locked around the chimney, I yelled for Kathe to call in the fire department to rescue me with extension ladders. But my neighbor, who was getting embarrassed for both of us, finally came over and talked me down.

In Wisconsin, I joined a party of hunters who expected me to climb way up in trees and stand for hours on portable stands—little nylon platforms exactly the size of my two Sorel boots. With no bench to sit on and *no* safety rails! Sheesh!

I dragged myself up into my stand the first morning with my heart thrashing in terror. I wish I could tell you what a triumph it was for me, getting up that high. I was at least ten feet above the ground, higher even than most stepladders.

Once up there, I spent the first hour with my arms clenched around the tree, wondering how I'd ever get my rifle up to me or how I'd get any bullets in it while I was squeezing the tree with both arms; or how, for that matter, I'd spot a deer when I was facing *in* toward the tree, my arms clamped around the trunk. To turn around, I'd have to loosen my grip on the tree, and *damned* if I was going to do that!

So I don't know how many 12-point bucks filed past my stand in the first hour of my hunt. I had my nose pressed up against the bark of the tree and wasn't able to see much behind me. You've heard the derisive term for ecologists: *tree huggers*. Well, I became a devout tree hugger, giving that poor pine a passionate embrace from which it will never recover. Somewhere west of Solon Springs there's a red pine with an hourglass figure from where a certain terrified guy squoze it one opening day.

I finally tied myself to the tree with a loop of rope so that when I fell off the stand the fall probably wouldn't be fatal. For the next hour or so I didn't give any thought to deer. I just struggled to control my vertigo. I finally got to the point where I could lean lightly against the safety rope and begin to peer around for deer.

"Okay, 12-pointer, I dare you to show your nose! This is *Grooms* on stand here! The ground before me is the Valley of Death. Set one cloven hoof in that lane and you're history, buck. You're cold, dead meat!"

Just then there came a sickening CRACK!!! and I found myself plunging down through space like Alice going down the rabbit hole. I came to an abrupt halt when the safety rope snapped taut under my armpits. I now know what it is like, *exactly*, to be hanged. In a split second I went from being an upright deer hunter to a terrified guy hanging from a tree, arms outstretched like a day-glo Christ on the cross, wondering whot-in-ell had happened.

The tree stand had disintegrated, is what had happened. I'll never know why. My friend Gary, who lent it to me, stood on it safely for five years without incident, and he's a great big galoot of an Irishman.

It took me some time to comprehend what had happened. My eyes were spinning and I was rather disoriented. I noticed, of course, that the deer stand wasn't beneath my Sorels supporting me.

With some adroit maneuvering, I finally got out of my rope and down off the tree without shooting myself. I was delighted to stand on terra firma the rest of the morning. Nobody ever fell *off* the ground.

At noon, I told my tale of woe to the others in my group. John, whose cabin we were staying in, said he had a good stand, a real honest-to-gosh wooden platform like I'd known in Minnesota. In fact, it overlooked the best site in the whole area from which a guy might ambush a 12-point buck. He generously offered it to me. How could I refuse?

His son added, "Yeah, it's a great stand! You just don't wanna get too near the edges!" I refused to contemplate that comment directly, though it foxed around in the back of my mind.

When I finally got to the "Ridge Stand," I understood. It was an itty-bitty piece of wood loosely attached to the *top* of a pine tree, almost two stories up in the air. Twice the height of my television antenna! As Mr. Bill used to put it so well, "Oh-*noooooooooo!*"

But I didn't want to come off as a total wimp. Not that I was worried about *my* reputation as a deer hunter, which has been hopelessly compromised. That I am the World's Worst Deer Hunter is documented, a matter of public record attested to by an abundance of witnesses from four states.

But my friend Gary, who had brought me into this hunt, is *the* deer hunting guru of our generation. Each year he shoots several deer with rifles, plus a few more with shotguns, archery gear, and black-powder muskets. His family eats venison three or four times a day. Gary writes about 40 how-to-gettum deer articles a year and has collaborated on one deer hunting book. He is the current reigning Mr. Expert Deer Hunter.

In view of all that, I didn't want our host, John, to learn that Gary's strange friend was a klutzy goose who was terrified of heights. I mean, that's pretty damn basic. John would have understood if I missed a deer or shot one in the tail or fell asleep and let four or five walk by my stand. That's ordinary incompetence. But it had never even *occurred* to John that I was such a cowardly bozo I wasn't even capable of climbing *into* his pet deer stand. That is extraordinary incompetence.

I wanted to cheat. If I stood near the base of the stand, I'd be safe and could always tell the gang I'd had a helluva hunt from the stand. But that Ridge Stand was so astonishingly high, there was no way to fake it. The stand was so high it was about as visible to hunters in the area as the sun. No way could I pretend to have used the stand if I didn't actually get up there.

So I clenched my deer hunting gear in my teeth and began to haul my trembling body up the tree. Halfway up, I had to stop to hang on and hyperventilate. The ground, blurry and distorted by my height, lay a giddy distance below.

I finally got on that little platform—the toughest thing I've done in years. I sat there clutching the platform, too sick with fear to even think about anything but my life insurance policy. From that height I could have killed a buck by lobbing nickels down on him.

Once I brushed the tiny log rail in front of me, and it FELL OFF! *"Aaargh! No railing, NO RAILING!"* So that's what the kid meant about not getting too near the edges. I told myself, "Whatever else you do, Mister White Hunter, *don't look down! Don't look down!"*

But just as I had in the morning, I began making progress on controlling my panic. After an hour of shuddering in horror, my mind began turning to 12-pointers with swollen necks.

Unfortunately, I had not slept well the night before, because I'd spent the night dreading climbing up into my little portable stand. Now I found myself dozing off. But since I was sitting on a shingle up in the clouds, each time I dozed off I went tipping toward the edge of my little platform. *Sheesh!* What a way to go: plummeting to your death in your sleep from a high-rise deer stand. I wouldn't even know I was dead until I was dead.

And that's when the wind came up. It didn't seem like much of a wind, actually, but it didn't need to be much to send me, the flagpole sitter, in motion. The top of the pine began to whip and sway, seven feet this way, nine feet that. And there I was—up there among the eagles without an airline barf bag. I realized that to shoot a deer I'd have to lead him by several feet, given how fast the treetop was moving.

I finally said, "That's it! I'm outta here! Bye-bye, tree stand! Hello, Mother Earth!"

Like I said, nobody ever fell *off* the ground, but I'm a good candidate to be the first guy to bring it off. I'll probably be deer hunting at the time.

Remembering the Brule River Tackle Supply

We who were close to it or worked there simply called it "the shop." The rest of the world knew it as the Brule River Tackle Supply. Located just east of Wisconsin's Bois Brule River, fabled river of voyageurs and presidents, the shop was a handsome cedar building that had been designed by its owner, John Rogers. Ostensibly, the purpose of the shop was to sell quality fly fishing tackle and related gear.

The shop was a special place. You saw that at once when you walked in. The cash register was an ornate piece of bronze sculpture with a hand crank and a satisfying bell. A relic from pre-inflation days, it could only conceive of purchases up to $59.99. The sale of an expensive item—an $800.00 canoe, say—occasioned an extended flurry of cranking and brassy dinging.

The walls were adorned with old sporting prints, stuffed trout, a skillet big enough to fry four dozen eggs, pre-1964 Winchesters, rawhide snowshoes, and photos of successful fishermen. A typewriter table carried a coffeepot and a dog-eared copy of *The Whole Earth Catalog*. Over the doors were the mounted heads of twin bear cubs. (After a break-in, John planned to put surveillance cameras in the cub heads, with fish-eye lenses planted in the eyeholes.) Slung overhead by thin cords was an 18-foot Old Town canvas canoe. Visitors were nervous about walking under it, though we shop clerks assured them that the canoe hadn't come crashing down "in two or three weeks."

Visiting fishermen were astonished to find that this backwoods shop stocked elegant equipment. We sold cane rods crafted by J.L. Leonard, Orvis, and the young firm of Thomas and Thomas. Our reels came from Hardy Brothers. We carried flies from Orvis and Bailey, though we were prouder of the custom creations from the vises of gifted local fly-tiers. Much of this gear transcended mere utilitarian status to become icons. I've watched fishermen wandering through the shop, speaking in whispers as though they were in church.

For two summers, Kathe and I and a cat named Pippin lived in the basement of the shop. Pippin earned his keep by mousing, although, truth to tell, he frogged as often as he moused. Kathe and I earned our checks by selling tackle, much of it to ourselves. We served as photo models for a mail-order catalog that was never printed. And we made desultory attempts to bring a measure of order to a business that refused to be organized.

The shop, you see, was never run according to conventional principles of merchandising.

We stocked many expensive items that rarely sold, while refusing to carry merchandise we knew would be profitable but which might lure the Wrong Sort of People to the shop. We mostly stocked products we *liked*.

Our business hours were erratic. Customers paced at the door in frustration, misled by notes promising we'd be "Back Soon." The notes always featured a sketch of a pop-eyed, happy trout with vibrating fins, done in the style of Ed Zern. Time was never very real to those of us who hung around the shop. A breakfast planned for daybreak usually went on the table late in the afternoon. By then we had all had a few beers and weren't concerned about the meal.

The shop's pricing system was also less than businesslike. Nothing carried a price tag, because we clerks wanted no limits on our freedom to charge what "felt right" at the moment. When a customer indicated interest in a product, we fumbled through catalogs to learn what others charged for that item. Then we'd prepare our offer. "Well, Dan Bailey gets $17.95 for that box," we'd explain, "but he does a volume we can't match. Our price has to be $18.13." Or: "Orvis would nick you $23.00 for that line, but (broad wink here) *you know Orvis! We* charge $19.76."

While we sold some equipment at normal markups, we frequently charged too little or too much, depending on our opinion of the customer. I once sold a Swedish compass at three times its full retail to a man who offended me. (He was a bizarre guy from the area who set his dogs' water troughs so high that the pack of curs could barely reach them. This was his genetic experiment to see if high water would cause dogs to give birth to long-legged puppies.) More typically, I sold a dozen flies at less than wholesale to a penniless graduate student just falling in love with fly fishing. In our small way, we used the shop to correct the unjust distribution of wealth in the world.

Nobody left our shop quite so confused as the fishermen who failed to see that we were a high-quality sporting goods store, not a backwoods bait store. A hundred times, maybe two hundred times, I've seen anglers approach John brusquely to ask, "Ya got *worms?*"

The answer was always the same, always delivered with the same timing. John would smile warmly and say, "Well you know, as a matter of fact I used to." Here there would be a pause . . . four beats. "But the doctor gave me a shot and now I'm just fine."

The fisherman's eyes would flit nervously as he backed out the door. Somehow he'd stepped through the Looking Glass into a world where bait stores were run by the Mad Hatter.

Some people called John crazy, yet those of us who loved the shop and its unique proprietor considered the Brule River Tackle Supply an island of sanity in a world gone mad. John's lanky frame, wild red beard, and idiosyncratic garb gave just a hint of the unusual mind that had created the shop. John was an artist, photographer, trout fishing guide, jazz drummer, business proprietor, and organic gardener.

And salesman. When the spirit was on him, John could sell smog to L.A. commuters. John was moved to eloquence once by the need to avoid the draft. He persuaded a local college to create the category of "Special Student" for him. John was the first and last Special Student they ever had, and he completed no courses. Though he started five projects for every one he finished, John brought a measure of greatness and individuality to everything he touched. He had style.

John once told us he'd never in his life read a book all the way through. Like a 20th-century aborigine, John had acquired his remarkable education exclusively through conversation. In art, John's tastes ran to the avant garde and abstract, but in everything else he was deeply distrustful of modernity. He swore the Germans had forgotten everything they knew about building a motorcyle after 1963, just as Detroit forgot how to make a decent car sometime in the 1940s. Setting himself against an increasingly plastic world, John filled his shop with canvas canoes, sturdy woolen clothing made for lumberjacks, shoes made for the Amish, hand-harvested wild rice, and fly rods crafted from bamboo.

I've said the shop was not a business in the usual sense. It's harder to say exactly what it was.

Perhaps it meant something a little different to each of us who were drawn to it. Some of us were serious about fly fishing, and the Brule had trout worth getting serious about. Other people came for the parties. When Kathe and I were graduate students, the shop was where we went to escape the tyranny of chopped-up time—the tedious march of semesters, mid-term exams and all that. In Brule the rhythms of time were set by the cycle of the seasons and the eternal slide of the river.

Mostly, the shop was a crossroads where people—all kinds of people—came and went.

Foremost among them was Gil, John's father. Gil was a retired salesman who missed schmoozing with customers and who consequently delighted in tending the shop. Whenever people stopped to ask what was happening on the Brule, Gil would blink with incredulity. "You don't *know*? You haven't *heard*? Jesus—the *whole damn thing is spilling into Lake Superior!*" The visitor would panic for a moment before remembering the Brule has been spilling into Lake Superior ever since the last glacier left, 11,000 years ago. Gil loved all jokes, but old jokes especially, and in his last years I think old jokes were among the best friends he had.

There were others. We regularly saw the college professor whose twin passions in life were Mozart and trout. And Owen spent time with us. Owen was a philosophy student hitchhiking across America to try to comprehend it. John picked him up along a Canadian highway because Owen did a slick soft-shoe routine while he thumbed.

There were the grand ladies and gentlemen, many of them

fabulously wealthy, who summered in the log-cabin mansions that graced the banks of the upper Brule. There were the young people—a mix of trout buffs, flower children, and the Good Time Charlies who were always having a party, planning a party, or recovering from yesterday's party. There was Glenn, the jet fighter pilot, who sometimes said "Hi!" by ripping off a series of barrel rolls a thousand feet above the shop roof. There was the dolorous old man, a religious fanatic from Maine, who wandered the nation on foot with all his belongings in a dirty handbag. He left home, he said, because he'd become disillusioned with Old Town canoes. He had walked out of the deep South heading for Chicago but, as he put it, "hit Eau Claire instead."

Some of these folks came for a weekend and stayed for years. Like a lamp in the darkness, John's personality drew unusual people from all over.

Although Kathe and I worked seven days a week in the shop, we missed little of the fishing on the Brule, for it was and is a night stream. The Brule's better trout spend sunlit hours lurking under cedar snags, venturing out to feed only when the sun drops below the river's western hills and the river is bathed in the diffuse light of the gloaming time. We would go out then, wading cautiously like herons or perhaps drifting in forest-green canoes, listening for the deep slurps that indicated a heavy trout was sucking May flies down through the surface film.

Since we could see nothing, we were obliged to cast toward the sound. Then the long rod would flash backward and forward, the line licking out like a snake's tongue into the dark to drop the fly delicately on the water. The fly would be of a traditional local pattern: an Arrowhead, perhaps, or the sensuous Antoine's Favorite, the drab but deadly Pass Lake, or maybe a deer-hair mouse complete with little leather ears and tail.

I often fished the river alone at night. If I did, I'd usually end up running the last hundred yards back to my car when the loneliness of the dark river had unraveled my nerves. I never feared any specific creature out there, but there's something fundamentally unsettling about wading a black river for hours and never hearing the voices of anything except coyotes, whippoorwills, and owls.

Coming back to the shop after such a night, it was indescribably pleasant to see the windows glowing with orange light, which meant a fire was leaping in the great fieldstone fireplace. I'd join the friends assembled around the fire in creaky wicker chairs. For hours into the night we'd tip bottles of beer and tell stories, the shop all dark but for the dancing fire, the world outside the windows all dark but for the lightning bugs flickering in fairy patterns over the dewy meadows.

Other nights we might decide impulsively to have a picnic and sleep the night on the sandy shores where the Brule empties into Lake Superior. Or sometimes we'd jump into John's "new" car, the '48 Ford with no license plates, and run down to Sylvia's resort for home-baked rolls.

Syl was as individual as John. When Syl talked about "the President," as she often did, she meant Coolidge. Syl baked for Coolidge during the summer—1928, I believe—when he made one of the Brule's great log lodges his White House. Coolidge infuriated other locals (but not Syl) at summer's end by rewarding them with autographed photos of himself instead of monetary tips.

Syl had a special way with children and other small animals. A woodchuck used to hibernate in her linen drawer, though from time to time he'd relocate to another spot in the house. Syl often took "Mike" out for guests, waving his bonelessly limp limbs to show how relaxed a woodchuck becomes in winter.

People were forever leaving stray kids with Sylvia. Once, hearing gunfire, Syl found some of her young guests pinging away with a .22 at a skunk that had jammed its head in a Mason jar. The panicked animal was now running around in circles by the garage. Syl stopped the shooting, scooped up the skunk, yanked the jar off its head, and released it. Without getting sprayed. A number of socially prominent and wealthy women came through the shop over the years; some were ladies and many were not. Syl was a lady.

For four years, the Brule and John's shop lay at the center of my outdoor life. Kathe and I returned to the river and the shop whenever our limited funds and the demands of our academic careers allowed us to.

We came for many reasons: because the Brule's mighty trout could sometimes be fooled with a fly; because old bourbon never tasted so good as when mixed with the sweet waters of the Brule; because the shop had merchandise we could find nowhere else; because over the river we might see eagles and ospreys locked in aerial combat; because only in Brule could we forget, if briefly, that on the far side of the globe American boys and Vietnamese boys were killing each other for no damn reason. John's shop and the river were a self-contained world where we could escape all that was mean about the world outside.

But all things pass.

Some of the people who frequented the shop moved away. Several relocated west near the blue-ribbon trout waters out there. Others drifted from trout fishing to other avocations. One, a pony-tailed backpacker whose preoccupation with gear seemed inconsistent with his anti-materialist ethic, now produces special effects for movie producer George Lucas.

Some of us, with varying degrees of deception, learned to pass ourselves off to the outside world as responsible adults. The most outrageous and chemically active couple from our circle got married when he became the district attorney for a northwoods community.

Several in the shop's circle died. Among them were two young individuals I counted as best friends, both struck down at an indecently early age. The stream of corny, predictable jokes flowing from Gil was finally stopped by cancer. One high-spirited young woman did not survive a collision with a tree when her boyfriend's motorcycle went airborne on a dark country road.

Some of us simply transferred the feelings we had for the Brule and the shop to other rivers, other sports, other shops, other people.

And John changed. Year by year, it became more difficult for him to manage the shop when his heart tugged toward other projects. He never had any stomach for dealing with rude customers, niggling bankers, and tax bureaucrats. In time, John's moral convictions evolved until he could not countenance the eating of meat or the killing of living things . . . and that didn't help him enjoy running a fly fishing shop. When his marriage dissolved, John let the shop go as part of the settlement.

Now, even the building is gone. Somehow the shop caught fire. One story has it that an unattended candle started the blaze down in the basement where Kathe, Pippin, and I had slept. Nobody knows for sure. Anyway, Kathe and I heard the building was leveled. I find it hard to believe any kind of fire could have taken down that wonderful stone fireplace, but we never found out. For ten years after the fire, Kathe and I were careful to travel nowhere near the Brule.

Yet we have never felt bitter about the abrupt loss of a place in which we'd spent so many happy hours. The destruction of the shop was painful and shocking . . . and yet not entirely unanticipated.

Most of us who were so fond of the shop, I suspect, were aware of a certain instability in the whole scene. That very fragility might have been part of its attraction. We were typical children of the 1960s, rebelling against our times; yet that very rebellion was part of the times. Thus the shop was not just a place but a time, and times cannot be frozen.

Mostly, though, I now understand that what was important about the shop was a certain state of mind. We were solemn about matters the world regards as trivial. We were silly about things the world takes seriously. In that sense, we will always remain employees of the Brule River Tackle Supply.

The Summer
of the Whippets Cap

I don't remember many details from the summer of the Whippets cap. A psychiatrist would say I didn't forget that stuff, I repressed it. Some things are simply too painful to hold in the mind. They burn through the fragile linings of the brain. But even though the fine points are forgotten, what I recall is hideous enough.

First, about the cap.

Just before that fishing season began, I bought a new lucky fishing cap. I'd been listening to public radio's *Prairie Home Companion*. The host, Garrison Keillor, often talked about Lake Wobegon, his mythical hometown, and its team, the Whippets. The Whippets were a truly woebegone team. They routinely lost to such teams as the Upsala Oof Dahs by scores of 42 to 3. Such a score would embarrass any football squad, but the Whippets were a *baseball* team!

As a promotional gimmick, my public radio station sold Whippets caps. They were blue, with a goofy dog face on the front. I bought one to make it my new fishing cap. It seemed a cute but harmless joke.

I wore my new fishing cap for the first time on a trout fishing jaunt in mid-May. It rained cats and dogs and I was forced to flee the stream, trout-less.

I wore the cap again a few days later on a return trip to the same stream. It wasn't a good day. No bugs hatched, no fish rose, and no trout ended up on my hooks. Well, it happens.

A week or two later, our family trailered my boat north to fish a walleye lake where friends own a cabin. The lake has a lot of walleyes in it, or so I'm told by the DNR. I want to check their creel census data sometime. It is also as clear as a swimming pool, and you can't catch a walleye there in daylight unless you fish with blasting caps. You fish at night or you fish in futility. We arrived too late on Friday to launch the boat for that night's fishing. On

Saturday a big birthday party kept me off the water during the evening bite. On Sunday we left about noon, walleye-less.

Back home, the Whippets cap and I went trout fishing again. It was too windy to cast.

My next fishing trip was to Lake Michigan. I brought along the Whippets cap. A friend and I arrived just a little too late to launch for the evening fishing. We hung around the landing, though, as boat after boat came in loaded down with 20-pound chinooks. In boat after boat, grinning anglers sat with salmon piled up almost as high as their knees.

But even as we stood there dripping envy, a cataclysmic west wind began to build. Lightning began popping all over the sky. Soon it was a real Fourth of July production. We spent the next day in the motel while Lake Michigan heaved about like a kid throwing a tantrum. When we finally could go fishing, the water had turned frigid and the fish were pouting. We eventually caught three cohos and a king, but I had expected more from four days of intense fishing.

I began to wonder how lucky my new fishing cap actually was.

Then came our family vacation, in early July. Kathe, my daughter Molly (then seven), and our two family dogs headed north to a resort along Lake Superior where we rented a cabin. The Whippets cap went along. But not far, for my trailer shredded a tire just north of Hinckley, one-third of the way to the lake. The station wagon was stuffed with clothes and beach toys, which left virtually no room inside where we could put gear from the boat. We removed just the most expensive and easily stolen equipment. I had to leave the boat and its other gear defended only by public morality while we returned home to get a new tire.

Two days later we had it. My boat was still there, which was a relief, although fretting about it had tied my stomach in knots. Our vacation began again.

On the evening we arrived at the lake, I launched and ran the boat up to the mouth of a river that pumps warm water into the big lake. Casting to such river mouths is the most productive way I've learned to fish Superior's North Shore. Wearing my lucky Whippets cap, I threw a Rooster Tail spinner into the jaws of a nine-pound lake trout. Alas, the fish twisted free just as we were netting it.

I didn't get upset. As I remember, I even laughed. How was I to know I had just experienced the pinnacle of my success for the rest of the summer? How could I know the lost laker was The Thrill of Victory and I could now look forward to several solid weeks of The Agony of Defeat?

The next day a warm breeze blew onshore, piling hot water up in the shallows. For three hours I pitched spinners at the river mouth before realizing the influx of warm water had sent the trout scooting for the cool depths. My deadly river-mouth technique was worthless. That afternoon, I trolled for five hours without getting a strike. My graph was eerily empty of fish.

The second day was virtually identical. Daylight river-mouth casting was fruitless. Then I trolled up and down the shore until my boat's hull wore a groove in the water. On my graph, I could see occasional fish angling up to inspect my lures. They all angled back down again, apparently contemptuous of my favorite lures.

I began to lose my sense of humor. When I came back in, the resort owner told me a lady tourist had taken a dandy laker casting from the shore.

Day three is a blur. I believe I casted from shore where the lady tourist had scored, then trolled the rest of the day. No hits. I won't bore you with all the details of the different lures, trolling patterns, speeds, depths, and other strategies I tried. I ran with attractors and fished "barefoot." I zig-zagged. I poured stinky goo on my lures from bottles printed with outlandish claims of irresistibility. I played around with setback lengths. I covered the spectrum of depths from 2 feet to 250 feet. Understand: I was *trying*.

Fishermen have a phrase for fishing like this. Ask how their fishing was and they say, "Well, the fishing was great. The catching wasn't much, but the *fishing* was great."

Ha, ha, ha! By that time, I was sick to my gills with "fishing." I wanted to do some *catching*. I wanted slime on my hands, blood on the bottom of the boat, a salmonid corpse in the cooler. I wanted to do a victory dance around the body of a fish. Any fish would do.

By this time, I could tell that Kathe and Molly were afraid of me.

If I entered a room, they would scurry out the other side. The dogs gave me a wide berth. My face was set in a scary glower. Our dinner conversations were somewhat tense, as I recall. Lunch and breakfast, too.

On the fourth day, Kathe and I tried a change of scene. We drove north to Grand Marais, borrowed a canoe from a friend, and spent a pleasant evening casting flies on a lake where the DNR claims to have stocked several thousand brook trout. I do want to check those stocking records sometime. We never saw a hint of fish life. The fishing was good, but the catching . . . was *shit!*

When we got home, we learned that a fantastic school of cohos had swum past the resort on Superior and "everybody" had limited out. The resort owner said, "They were hitting so fast you couldn't get a second line in the water before another coho would be on the first line." He was irked with me for having given up on Superior, I thought, and he grinned as he twisted the knife in my guts.

By morning the winds changed, the water temperatures plummeted, and the cohos had disappeared somewhere into the vast oblivion of Lake Superior. I trolled up and down the shore, washing the paint off my lures.

By this time my disposition had become less buoyant, and Kathe would not enter the boat with me. She met a fellow along the shore reading a Dickens novel. He had a rod baited with dead smelt that he just pitched out on the bottom. He caught three lakers while Kathe watched—and while I trolled in furious frustration in my boat, with its several thousand dollars of electronic gear and three tackle boxes full of lures whose worth I am afraid to calculate.

Let me briefly explain what this all meant to me. Nobody enjoys getting skunked. Nobody *likes* getting skunked several days in a row. So several weeks of spectacular futility might test the soul of any angler. If that angler is well-equipped and (*ahem!*) modestly accomplished, several consecutive weeks of totally fish-less fishing are apt to feel bad. And if that same angler occasionally shares his expertise in print—if in fact he is the Great Lakes columnist for a certain widely respected national publication—well, in such a case THE WORST FISHING SLUMP IN THE HISTORY OF

HUMANKIND IS APT TO GO DOWN A LITTLE HARD!

It did. I brooded and fumed. I had bags under my eyes. I was beyond civil speech. Was somebody punishing me for my sins? While I'm far from perfect, I've never come close to sinning enough to deserve such agony. To tell the truth, once—just once—I'd *love* to sin enough to merit this kind of retribution.

I gave serious thought to making an animal sacrifice to the Red Gods, in order to lift the curse. A certain yapping "Yorkie-Poo" owned by a couple from Illinois suggested itself as an appropriate offering. I hoped the gods wouldn't insist that I sacrifice one of my own dogs.

The last day of our vacation was my weirdest ever on Superior. Offshore winds had filled the lake with army tentworms until the lake seemed frosted with fuzzy yellow bugs. Seagulls sat in the bug slick, getting fat and burping as they slurped insects.

When I turned on my graph, I learned that the water beneath the bug slick was filled with fish from top to bottom. They were stacked like sardines below the bugs—thousands of trout, more trout than I believed lived in Superior.

But they wouldn't hit a lure. I fished behind cowbells and dodgers and flashers. I fished lures without attractors. I tried long-lining and downrigging. I used diving planers and planer boards. The fishing was great, but the catching . . .

Oh, but I was canny—versatile and persistent. I spent an hour drifting into the bug slick as silently as a gull, casting into the fish. They weren't buying. Then for two hours I jigged them, using every jigging technique known to man plus some never before tried. Not one trout so much as put a lip on my lures. The main surprise is that I never managed to foul-hook a trout; they must have been moving just enough to keep free of my hooks.

Thus ended our vacation. I was a giddy, whimpering shell of a man as I drove home. Here comes Steve Grooms, the ultimate fish conservationist. In his ultimate respect for the sanctity of life, he's gone beyond catch and release; he leaves out the catching part. You could say my confidence was down. I didn't at that moment believe I could successfully get a fish by walking into a fish market and offering cash for one.

Shall I tell you about my big fishing trip to Nebraska later that summer? Or my October trophy walleye trip to Canada? No. You're not stupid. You can fill in the blanks—and blanks they were.

But you want to know about the Whippets cap? Did its curse ever lift? Really! What curse? Do you think the *hat* was truly unlucky? Ha! I am a scientific modern angler, not a superstitious person. I walk under ladders and request hotel rooms on the thirteenth floor. Right?

But anybody can see a *pattern* when it's that obvious. I'm sure there is nothing wrong with my lucky fishing cap that couldn't be set right by a team of four or five experienced exorcists. That damned cap hangs on a hook in my basement now, 232 miles from my boat. And that's as close as it's ever going to get.

The Field Tester
for Chippewa Pride

Exactly where to begin any story is an arbitrary decision. We might as well begin this one on that muggy June evening on Wisconsin's Kinnikinnick River, when I was in my first summer of fly fishing. I never made a cast that night, for the May fly hatch I intended to fish didn't "come off."

Which was a big relief. Catching a fish would have been fun, but my aspirations were realistically modest. The failure of the hatch had saved me from the usual embarrassment of screwing up good chances. I had caught nothing, but for once it wasn't my fault.

The only excitement came when some hellish creature flew out of the dark to attack my face. I brushed it away. It came back. I whapped it away. It came back. Whinnying with terror, I began swatting furiously. It finally dawned on me that I was having a boxing match with my own fly as it dangled from my rod tip.

Back at the car, casing my rod, I met a friendly fellow just coming off the river. Out of politeness, I asked how he'd done. "Not too shabby." He'd caught nine trout, including a 19-incher. And this happened two pools upstream from where I'd spent the evening swatting mosquitoes . . . and my own fly.

I suddenly saw that there was more to fly fishing for trout than I'd previously wanted to admit. I understood that my frequent "bad luck" was plain old bad fishing. Though I had a reputation as a reasonably skillful bass and pike angler, I was a trout-fishing stooge. That night, I vowed to become competent.

Competence did not arrive overnight.

For one thing, the Wisconsin trout waters near my home are not easy to fish. Our streams are confined, clear, and slow. Casting is tricky in the narrow lanes of air between box elder limbs and overhanging thatches of canary grass. Since our insects are small, we fish with thread-like leaders and midget flies. Our trout are streamborn browns with eyes like macro lenses and no sense of whimsy when inspecting a clumsily tied artificial.

On my own, I was no more threatening to these trout than the gaily colored warblers flitting in the streamside trees. But I met a group of skillful anglers who had already worked out the challenges of midwestern trout waters. These experts befriended Kathe and me. They were willing to share their hard-earned wisdom.

My mentors were impressive people. Three eventually wrote sophisticated articles for national fly fishing magazines. Two were graduate students in entomology who assigned Latin names to what I called "bugs." Tall, charismatic Gary was our acknowledged leader and theoretician. A fellow named Dave looked *just* like Mark Trail and dispensed *bon mots* of expertise with insouciant confidence. Mike fished one or another of our streams every day of the season and knew them inch-by-inch, trout-by-trout. Butch combined astonishing casting skills with an uncanny ability to choose an odd-ball fly that would be irresistible to a trout. Old Ben fished exclusively at night for trophy fish with strange, lead-loaded flies that were as lethal as a gill net. Curt, the fire fighter, also specialized in catching huge browns; and if you asked him how, the answer was always: "I slipped a Muddler to 'im."

These men seemed to stride the streams like gods. They pulled mighty trout from hard-fished pools where ordinary anglers struggled to fool six-inchers. These superb anglers were the stuff of legends.

I worshipped them. I longed to *be* one of them. I fantasized about the day when other anglers would pause to point reverently to the pool "where Grooms took the seven-pounder on that little caddis pattern he always uses."

The first year or two of my apprenticeship was sheer joy. I bumbled along at the heels of my mentors with puppyish enthusiasm. They never mocked my ineptness, though the only fishing knot I could tie consistently was the wind knot. My expert friends showered me with praise when I found a trout so gullible it ate one of the Frankensteinian products of my fly-tier's vise.

The Troubles didn't appear until I began to get the hang of the sport. The price of growing proficiency was rising expectations, both my own and my sense of what others expected of me.

Once it was a thrill to fish without getting skunked, but that innocent delight soon faded. I began to feel a failure if I caught fewer trout than I "should" have, given the circumstances. Trout fishing was still fun, mostly. But increasingly I came to dread the inevitable *"It was good for me, was it good for you?"* discussions with friends after an evening of fishing. I fished harder and harder, always with the sense of not measuring up.

Soon I was not fishing for myself at all but, rather, fishing so I'd have trout to report when my buddies asked how I'd done. A private sport had become a type of public competition that was fiendishly frustrating because I was competing against the rubber yardstick of my friends' success as they fished nearby pools out of my sight.

I learned, on a day when I caught six trout, that I should be ashamed; if the fish were being *that* stupid, Gary would have taken two dozen. If I boasted of the 12-incher I'd just caught, Mike would report two 16-inchers the same evening. I had never *seen* a 16-incher—not knowingly, anyway—much less caught one.

With misery, I realized that my mentors had little regard for small trout, the eager beavers I concentrated my fishing on. To win respect, I'd have to catch a trout with heft. I was forced, much against my will, into fishing at night, for that's the only time a hefty brown in our waters can be tricked into doing something silly.

At first I took at face value the success stories my friends told. My own exploits were exaggerated with careful calculation. Scruples (and a fear of being found out) kept me from claiming a 15-incher unless it went at least 12 inches. In the presence of witnesses, however, when I caught a 13-incher I called it a 10-incher, to foster the fiction that *Grooms* didn't stretch his trout.

Once I discovered that one of my mentors measured his fish against an old canvas creel that had shrunk until it added two inches to a trout. What a delicious, smug feeling that discovery brought, like learning your minister cheats on his income taxes even more than you do. After that, I grew cynically suspicious of notable catches that were witnessed only by whippoorwills.

Alas, as I worked my way up the ladder of trout fishing competence, I became a thorough snob about the cruder souls still clinging to lower rungs. My friends and I poked endless fun at the cretins who fished for coarser fish than trout with coarser tackle than cane fly rods and tiny flies. We printed a satirical and scatological newsletter that mocked the ding-a-lings who fished with spincast reels, suggesting they caught their "browns" by angling ice-fishing style down the holes of outhouses.

Of course, our group sniffed with revulsion at anyone who kept an occasional trout for supper. "He *kills* trout," we'd say, in a tone of voice appropriate for reference to child molesters.

Ultimately, I perceived that my friends didn't even respect all catch-and-release anglers who fished for trout with small flies and bamboo rods. I heard them saying—even, dear God, heard *myself* saying: "Sure he catches trout, but the only thing he knows is dragging nymphs around on bottom all day." We made snide comments about the fellow who used garish attractor fly patterns during hatches he couldn't match "the right way" with flies that successfully imitated natural bugs.

But, though I became as catty as the most arrogant of my mentors, I had a problem. After three years of being an apprentice expert, I was not significantly more skillful than the doltish anglers we scorned. If I didn't emerge as a competent angler, and damned soon, I'd become known as a fellow who hung around with good fly fishers but was not one. Bumbling is acceptable, even cute, when it's seen as a stage one is working through. In time, it becomes one's fixed place in the trout fishing hierarchy.

I prepared for my fourth fly fishing season with a keen sense of desperation. That winter, I schemed. I read several how-to books. I invented some new fly patterns to match the Hendrickson May fly. I bought a new, longer rod, working on the theory that "more is better." I practiced the power of positive thinking.

Our group opened the season that year on the Namekagon River. It's a lovely river whose banks in May are usually lined with butter-yellow marsh marigolds. Ernie Schweibert fished there and later rhapsodized about the river. I know, Ernie *always* rhapsodizes, but the Namekagon is beautiful. Though other streams have more trout, the Namekagon is roomy enough to permit comfortable casting, even among the crowds of opening day.

That weekend I could do no wrong. My new Hendrickson patterns were deadly. The new rod gave me more reach. I fished with the intensity of a bass tournament pro. For the first time in my life, people came to *me* to ask what flies were working. After three days, not only had I caught more fish than anyone, but our biggest brown was a 16-incher I took in a blizzard-like Hendrickson hatch in the Lover's Pool.

Fishing in the waning light of that last day, I felt redeemed. In a few minutes we'd go home, and I could bask in the glory of my remarkable weekend. The bungler had come of age.

Then, one pool below me, Gary took a seventeen-inch trout. I was livid. Couldn't the gods of fishing let me be the high rod once in my life? I snapped out a *"Damn!"* loud enough for everyone to hear.

That curse echoed in my mind for weeks afterward. What, I asked, is wrong with me? How could the success of a good friend move me to fury? That was *sick.* Something was very wrong with my soul. Even I could see that.

Weeks later, Kathe and I left our shabby student apartment in Minneapolis and moved to Wisconsin to spend the summer working in a fly fishing shop near the Brule River.

Life in Brule was nothing like life in the city and the joyless graduate school we had left. Daisies, Indian paintbrush, and buttercups bloomed in the lush green fields around the shop. One night the aurora borealis wrapped the whole sky in shimmering green-and-rose curtains of neon light. Kathe and I lost the compulsion to read newspapers. We slipped into a new kind of time. We began moving more deliberately and speaking in gentler voices. We forgot to wind our watches. We had beer for breakfast.

From such a perspective, some of the anglers who came through the shop amused us with their feverish compulsion to catch trout. One—I'll call him Al—was a member of our fishing group from home. He dropped by the shop one day to boast about the dandy trout he'd taken on the *Tricorythodes* hatch that morning from the Sucker Lake stretch of the Brule. He'd caught several 14-inchers.

Or so he said.

I was furious, though I hid that fact. For one thing, I'd learned that Al had lied to me several weeks ago about two 17-inch trout he'd caught on one of our home streams. Following his detailed instructions, I'd flogged a piece of water to a lather, hoping to catch trout like those. Then I learned that Al's instructions had sent me 16 miles from where he had actually caught the fish—and to the wrong river, no less!

Moreover, I had fished the "Trico" hatch on Sucker Lake several times without ever seeing a trout over ten inches. I *knew* he was lying. Again.

When I offered to fish Sucker Lake with Al the next morning, what I really meant was, "I'm calling your bluff, you pretentious goose." I'd be the winner either way. Either Al would show me where I could catch good fish for the rest of the summer, or I'd show Al up as the fork-tongued scumbag I already knew him to be. Either result would have pleased me equally.

On that same day, a local brewery debuted a new beer label. Back then we believed a brewmaster would put out his finest product when a label was new. Then, once it had won a following, we figured he'd cheapen the product and go back to producing the usual swill. So on the night before my showdown with Al, several of us volunteered to become field testers for this new Chippewa Pride beer. Two cases disappeared quickly.

In spite of our indiscretions, Al and I rose in time to suit up and step into the water just as the first flush of dawn glowed over the eastern bank of Sucker Lake. The "lake" is just a wide spot in the Brule, capped by frisky rapids at both ends. Ranks of Norway and white pines ascend the steep valley walls, and fragrant cedars line the banks. The better trout skulk under the sweepers and scum patches by day. They don't show their noses when sun is on the water and they regard dinky May flies, like Tricos, with supercilious contempt.

Al and I began working upstream from the foot of the lake, he on the left, I on the right. We moved silently, locked in a competition so bitter that neither of us dared acknowledge it. I was delighted to see no 14-inchers rising. As I'd expected, the river was filled with little brookies and baby browns bashing Tricos with the typical exuberance of small trout.

Then I was jolted to hear Al's voice over the merry gurgle of the Brule. He was talking to the trout. "Come on, you little fucker! Take it, now. *Take it, take it, take it!* Awwww, *damn* you! *Take that fucking fly!*"

I was shocked. Did Al always have such an antagonistic relationship with trout, or was this a by-product of our feud? These were just fish, after all, innocent and lovely little fish that were simply going about the daily business of survival. Their only crime was being small. They had done nothing to earn such contempt.

Then my mind was jerked back to more compelling considerations. Last night's bottles of Chippewa Pride had made an evil brew in my bowels that now wanted out—that now *insisted* on coming out. With every few steps, I was bent double by a belly spasm. It was a bad time to be wearing waders.

At the head of Sucker Lake lies a great boulder that clumsy canoeists usually beach up on as they career out of the rapids above. Current sweeping around that boulder has scoured out a pocket of dark, deep water. I suddenly recognized that as the only spot in Sucker Lake where a nice trout might be taken that morning.

Al obviously had the same idea. (Suppose the sumbitch *had* taken a 14-incher here yesterday!) We began to wade faster as we both homed in on that rock, whipping our flies out over the water with vicious intensity. I was going to reach the boulder before Al did if it killed me.

Suddenly, it was clear that I would pay a gruesome price for my pride if I didn't get out of the river immediately. Abandoning all dignity, I lurched toward the bank, threw my rod into a cedar, and hobbled into the woods. I yanked down my waders and pants and got behind an alder just in time.

There, I had several minutes to contemplate the nasty scene I'd helped create that morning.

Rarely can we identify a single moment when our character is forever changed, when the human spirit rises like a repulsive nymph surging out of the silt to become reincarnated as a proud-winged creature of the air. But the man who emerged sheepishly from the brush that morning was not the same fellow who had bolted into it moments earlier.

I suddenly understood that the mess I'd made in the woods was not nearly as ugly as the spectacle of two men using trout to club each other's strutting egos. Perhaps Al had lied. Perhaps he had developed a grotesque relationship with trout fishing. Well, so had I. I no longer cared about his character flaws, as I had more than enough of my own to deal with. For years I had fretted about becoming recognized as a competent trout fisherman. I should, instead, have been fretting about why *that* seemed so important.

That was many years ago. I have a new mentor now, the widow of one of the expert anglers I sought to emulate. Gary taught me how to catch trout; Jan teaches me how to enjoy trout fishing. Jan always comes back from the stream grinning and bubbling over with stories. If you ask her how she did, she doesn't respond by boasting about the size of her fish, even though she often catches trout worth boasting about. Instead, her answer is always, "Oh, I had a *great day!*" And she means it.

It seems so simple now. The only sensible definition of a "good fisherman" is someone who consistently takes delight in his or her fishing. How could I ever have thought otherwise? In those terms, if only in those terms, I am as competent as I ever dreamed of being.

It is enough.

The Editor

For over six years, I was the senior editor of a regional outdoor magazine called *Fins and Feathers*. We managed to put out an entertaining magazine that is still remembered fondly by at least several dozen readers and the parents of frequent contributors. But it wasn't a very glamorous deal. Seen from the inside, making outdoor magazines is like making sausage. You really don't want to look too closely.

In the early years our "office" was a decrepit farmhouse that would have flunked any building code ever written. Squirrels lived inside the walls back by the kitchen. When they fought or made baby squirrels, the thumping was distracting. Wintertime indoor temperatures were so low that our breath sometimes formed visible plumes. I often worked wearing a down parka and, when not typing, gloves.

The toilet was a particular source of aggravation. It was situated just around the corner from my desk and was unusually loud. It concluded each thunderous flush with a long scatological hoot (I always thought it was saying, "*WHEEEE! I saw what you just did!*"). The only furniture in the waiting room was the third seat of the publisher's Volkswagen van, which had been removed and propped up on a shaky pile of boards right beside the bathroom.

Now and then, some misguided soul in a *suit* would show up, hoping to do business with this new magazine. Such people were mostly salesmen on commission who wouldn't have come near the place if they'd known what the bank knew about our finances. One fellow, thinking the magazine was *Fans and Feathers*, showed up hoping we dealt in kinky sex aids.

A few visitors came asking to meet the senior editor—me. If I happened to be in the bathroom when they arrived, through the door I'd hear a co-worker say, "Mr. Grooms is away from his desk, but he'll be right with you." Then I'd get to make my entrance as Archie Bunker so often did, with a gurgling *Ka-whoosh, snarkle, snarkle, WHEEEEE!*, emerging from the bathroom spraying deodorizer with my left hand while offering my right for a firm handshake.

The editorial budget was tight. We offered too little money and paid too late to allow us to do business with professionals—with people who knew what they were doing, in other words. Which meant I had to find enough material to fill a magazine once a month from amateurs working for the glory of having their work appear in print. We ran stories written by truck drivers, hungry "pro" anglers who hadn't made their mark yet, high school kids, and semi-literate fishing guides. I bought photos from photographers who had just purchased cameras and weren't sure what all the confusing little gizmos were supposed to do.

One aspiring wildlife artist was eager to paint a deer on the cover for us, just for the publishing credit. I was delighted until I saw his work, a painting of two brown mammals with a passing resemblance to whitetails. "Deer don't look like little Arabian stallions with antlers," I objected. "They look like big *goats* with antlers." The painter folded his arms across his chest and told me I was nuts. I began pulling photos of deer from our file. "See!" I exulted. "Goats! They look like goats!"

The painter finally cracked after I'd slapped down sixteen goatish deer photos. "I don't give a damn *what* they look like," he howled over his shoulder as he left. "I'm an *artist!*"

The obscurity and regional appeal of our magazine gave us freedom to do things that would have been politically unacceptable at more successful magazines. If *Outdoor Life* took a progressive stand on a controversial conservation issue, for example, it might lose several thousand readers. We didn't have several thousand readers in those days, so we pretty much said what we pleased.

I was probably the first editor in the history of the "hook 'n' bullet" press who had strong feminist convictions. I frequently ran pictures of women hunting and fishing along with men, which was fairly radical at the time. But my clandestine ambition was to print a how-to fishing article written by a woman. To my knowledge, it had never been done. Printing such a story would be a blow for women's liberation, or at least a sneak punch.

There was one hitch. I couldn't find a woman who could write outdoor stuff like a man. Every woman writer I located only confirmed all the stereotypes about women that I meant to shatter. "I went fishing with my crazy husband once, and he tried to make me put a hook in a yucky *leech!*"

Then I learned a major tackle manufacturer had a woman outdoor writer on its Expert Council, and (this was too good to be true!) she lived just miles from me. Her name was something like "Joan Lovestud." I now suspect that this was a pen name chosen with feminine guile, but at the time I missed the point.

I phoned Ms. Lovestud to request a how-to fishing story. I reassured her, "We don't condescend to women at *Fins and Feathers*. I mean, you don't have to include photos of yourself in a tight sweater to sell a story to *us*."

The lady writer sounded dubious but interested. She asked to meet me at her home.

The woman who met me at the door was an aging floozie with peroxided hair and eyebrows that she'd drawn on skin with a grease pencil. She had once been a beauty of the lollapalooza type. Think of Jayne Mansfield twenty years past her prime, Dorothy Malone a little long in the tooth, Diana Dors in her cellulite years.

The first thing I saw upon entering her home was a huge photo of the lady writer in a sweater that was stretched to the tensile limits of yarn. The sweater was three sizes too small, or the breasts three sizes too large, I couldn't tell. It was *exactly* the photo I had told her she needn't use to sell an article to me.

Ms. Lovestud had included that photo, I later learned, with every article she ever submitted to outdoor editors (who were all male, of course). It was upon the impact of this photo that she had built her writing career. A fellow outdoor writer later told me Ms. Lovestud had other ways of cultivating favor with male editors and wasn't too fastidious to use them.

In short, she wasn't the ideal candidate to advance the cause of feminism in outdoor writing. Her articles advised lady anglers to coordinate their outfits with the color of their rods. "Girls, you don't need to sacrifice your femininity just to go fishing," she wrote.

"Put flower decals on your waders."

From the earliest days of the magazine, the process of putting each month's issue together was a tear-your-hair-out crisis. Our composition procedures remained embarrassingly amateurish even after the magazine had grown in size and accumulated a considerable number of readers.

For example, we never felt we had the luxury of taking time to proofread. As fast as copy came out of our typesetting machine, it was slapped on the layout boards—hot, wet, and riddled with glitches. More than once, the publisher's van bumped down the road toward the printing shop with someone in the back frantically gluing down strips of copy. Although I had no journalism training, I was pretty sure that this wasn't how they made magazines at *Sports Afield.*

Our sloppiness began to bug me. Typos and other boo-boos showed up with increasing frequency as the workload got larger and the staff did not. I once dashed off a headline for a camping article about cooking over an open fire. In my haste, I wrote: "Camping Over An Open Fire." A snotty reader wrote to suggest that the practice might be uncomfortable. Picky, picky, picky!

Quality control problems extended to the pictures. Some of our pictures looked like they'd been printed with a potato instead of a printing plate. Photo captions would routinely be switched, so a caption identifying *The author on his favorite deer stand* would appear under a picture of an albino squirrel. Or photos were "flopped," resulting in pictures of anglers in caps promoting "nertS" fishing line and T-shirts proclaiming they were "kcabrozaR sasnakrA" fans. Pictures of jigs almost always ran upside down, as if lead floated. Once a year we ran a photo of saugers with a caption calling them walleyes; once a year we got a bitchy letter from the one reader (a sarcastic biologist) who knew the difference.

Our early stabs at four-color pictures were humiliating. At a time when color separations were being done at other magazines by technicians with computers and lasers, we had a little mustachioed guy with a camera who used his broom closet for a darkroom. Our most notorious cover was an artistic still-life that featured a rustic barn-wood background, a fine old shotgun, and three plump blue-head mallards (a species never seen before nor since).

My anxiety about quality control was peaking at about the time we printed our famous story on bow hunting for carp. That story concluded, "Be sure to equip yourself with stout gear because you need a strong string to handle 35 *pounds of thrashing crap*"! (Which is probably true, but it's not quite what we'd intended.)

I threw a fit. Our typesetter, a flower child with long hair and an attitude, was proud of her speed but took offense at requests for accuracy. She maintained that the magazine needed her more than she needed us, and she was right. At my outburst over the "thrashing crap" typo, the typesetter argued, "Only one letter was wrong."

"But we write about *ducks* in every issue," I howled. "Think about that!"

I seized a layout board for the next issue. "We've gotta start proofing this stuff," I roared. To further press my point, I added, "I bet I can find something wrong with the very first page I check!" It didn't take long. In letters an inch high, we promised the story, "HUNTING ILLINOIS' HOME-GROWN HONKIES"!

The most memorable story ever sent to me came from a fellow who had "taken to the woods" to make a living by trapping and writing outdoor stuff. I liked Jim and assigned him a series of wildlife portraits. But the first articles he sent me were drab, full of encyclopedia information about such things as the home range of the white-footed deer mouse and the gestation period of screech owls. I urged him to spice up his copy with personal anecdotes.

Jim's next story, about weasels, followed my directions with a vengeance. It began:

> Even in a deer camp, sooner or later a guy has to take a bath. Larry, hunting with us six years ago, finally got to that point. But he didn't know there was a weasel living in our deer shack. When Larry peeled off his longies, the weasel leaped out from under the bed and attached itself to that part of his anatomy most resembling a mouse.

The story went on to relate how Larry absolutely could not unfasten the weasel, how his screams attracted other hunters who clubbed it (the weasel) to death, and how Larry was rushed off to an emergency room. In fact, his rifle had to be mailed home by the rest of the gang because Larry had lost a fair amount of blood and was unable to walk.

Well, I just couldn't print it. No one, no *man* at least, could read that anecdote and then pay the least attention to anything else in the magazine. That story would leap right out at the reader . . . sorta like the weasel.

It was the only thing I censored from a story in six years as an outdoor editor.

We got interesting phone calls. Our secretaries often told callers, "Just flush 'em down the toilet." Without asking, I knew that the callers had dead guppies and were seeking our advice on how to dispose of them. I never knew how often guppies died until I worked at an outdoor magazine. After talking it over in a staff meeting, we told the secretaries to recommend burial at sea without bothering the editors with more guppie calls.

One lady called to report in a testy voice that some ducks were still loitering around (it was winter) and they were supposed to be in Louisiana or some damn place. She demanded to know what I intended to do about that. I just asked her if the ducks had wings, which didn't make her any happier.

Nor did I please the guy who called to boast that he'd just shot what he figured was the new World-Record Cottontail Rabbit. He wanted me to tell him how he could get some fame for that. Because cottontails are notoriously weak in the antler department, I didn't know how he could work up a Boone and Crockett score on his jumbo bunny.

Another caller told me that a hawk had been beating up a dove. In fact, the wounded dove was huddled on the sill of her front window with the glowering hawk perched in a nearby maple, waiting to finish the job. She hoped I knew a place where she could have the dove healed at no cost to her. I drew a blank before remembering the Raptor Center at the University of Minnesota. If the dove staged a rally and busted up the hawk, I told her, she could go there to get the hawk fixed for free.

I felt bad about the caller who had a pail full of fish that were barking at him. He wondered what they were. Well, if they began *meowing*, I said, they were probably catfish. An hour after he hung up on me I remembered that freshwater drum, a rough fish, make a sound like barking.

The phone rang off its hook when we ran my article, "How to Pick an Opening Day Walleye Lake." I described getting skunked one cold walleye opener until our party got off the big lake we were fishing and moved to a shallow lake that warmed up faster each spring. The article had photos of the limits of walleyes some fellow staffers and I had caught after using our heads and picking the right sort of lake.

Reader after reader called to say, "Gee, that lake looks awful familiar. I think that's where I went to Scout camp. I just can't remember the name." *Three* callers said the lake looked just like where grandma used to have her cabin only, doggone, they'd forgotten the name of the lake.

They didn't fool me for a second with those hokey stories. Those creeps didn't want to learn how to pick an opening-day lake by using their heads. They just wanted the name of the lake where we'd done well.

I told them. I even told them just where it was. Then I added, "But you don't want to go there. After we limited out, the Brainerd area guides moved in on Pine Mountain Lake like a pack of hyenas. There probably aren't two walleyes left in the lake." (Hey guys, if you're reading this now, I admit it: *That* was a bald-faced lie!)

One of the bigger mistakes I made was buying a fancy fishing boat. It was a state-of-the-art craft equipped with a live well, three sonar units, trolling motors fore and aft, and a whole lot of other gear I didn't know how to use. I think the idea was to prove to readers that *Fins and Feathers* was "on the water" pursuing the cutting edge of fishing technique. Buying the boat wasn't such a bad idea—just a tad pretentious—but I really goofed when I painted the magazine's logo in ten-inch-high letters on each side.

The first time I launched that boat, I got distracted by all the information pouring out of my sonar gear. With my eyes on the graph, I ran my fancy boat right into the side of a boat innocently anchored near the landing. This collision occurred on the busy opening of walleye season, so about three dozen boats witnessed the ramming. And because of the ten-inch letters, they knew just who had done it. Those anglers learned that *Fins and Feathers* was on the water, all right; and until it got off again, life out there wouldn't be safe.

It got worse. Everywhere I went, people stared at me in my hot-shot boat. If they were expert anglers, they giggled to see me fishing in dumb places with dumb tactics. If they were inept, they followed me around like trusting puppies, trying to discover my secret fishing holes. That made it tricky for me to follow them to *their* secret fishing holes.

But nothing quite matched the Sunday I launched my boat in Lake Michigan out of the port of Kewaunee, Wisconsin. My partner was my English professor friend, Charlie. We had already put in three marathon days of fishing, averaging four hours of sleep a night. A guy can do that when he's young and foolish, although Charlie and I were mighty wobbly when we hit the water that last morning.

Sunday turned out to be one of those cold-front days with indigo skies and mile-high, cotton-candy clouds . . . beautiful for every-thing except fishing. Since the weather was so nice, about 200 boats circled in a giant pack in front of the pier. Threading a path through all that traffic was so tricky I had no trouble keeping awake. I was determined not to ram anybody with so many witnesses.

Nobody was catching fish. I knew that for a fact, because on such days nobody has anything better to do than watch other boats. All morning long, 200 boats circulated while bored anglers studied each other through binoculars. Every time somebody touched a rod, anglers in 199 other boats went nuts before finally concluding, "Ah hell, that's no fish. He's just changing lures."

Then one of our downrigger rods fired. I recall the lure: a little green Andy Reeker that had never taken a fish before and never would again. Charlie was eager to fight a fish; he stood up in the bow laughing gleefully while the rod thrashed like a whip. I ran around the boat clearing the other lines and bringing in gear that might interfere with the fight.

Charlie tussled with the twenty-pound Chinook salmon for about fifteen dramatic minutes. The fish jumped four or five times and made several drag-burning runs. Charlie finally muscled the salmon all the way to the back of the boat. I had the net almost around it when—*patooie!*—the Andy Reeker popped free and grazed my cheek as it shot by.

Charlie dropped the rod and stared at me with a look of horror on his face. "Oh God," he wailed. "I feel terrible!" For some reason, Charlie always lashed himself mercilessly after losing a fish. But this time he seemed unusually distressed.

"Charlie," I said, "it wasn't your fault! The hook just popped out."

"You don't understand! I feel *wretched!*"

"Lighten up, Charlie! It could have happened to anybody!"

"No, I mean I feel horrible! I gotta TAKE A SHIT! Right NOW!"

"You *whaaaa?* Charlie, I've got three sonars on this boat, but I don't got a toilet!"

"Then I'm gonna *HANG IT OUT OVER THE SIDE!*"

Charlie ran to the bow and did just what he'd threatened to do. Moments later, brown objects began bobbing up by the motor and went twirling dreamily in our stern wake. I slumped down in my seat until my eyes were barely higher than the gunwales, trying to run the boat through traffic while making myself unrecognizable.

But what was the use? I knew the anglers in 199 other boats had spent five hours watching the fancy *Fins and Feathers* boat, monitoring our every move through binoculars. They'd cheered when our boat hooked the only salmon of the morning. They'd groaned when Charlie's rod went limp. And then, with mounting astonishment, anglers in 199 other boats had observed the next developments on the *Fins and Feathers* boat.

I motored right back to the landing, drove home, and slept for 13 hours. The first thing I did upon waking was to paint over that accursed logo.

It wasn't always better when I fished in other people's boats, especially when I found myself with guys determined to demonstrate their prowess for the celebrity outdoor editor. Although it happened many times, the most memorable such trip was the first time I fished with Tom. Tom, an ebullient and talkative Dutchman with arms like Popeye the Sailor Man, was a truly accomplished angler. Unlike some of my other fishing partners, Tom had a lot of prowess to show off.

While Tom was remarkable for his skills, I was even more impressed by his ferocious drive to catch fish. The day before he got married, Tom sat his fiance down for a heart-to-heart talk. "In my life," he told her, "fishing and hunting are Number One and Two. You are Number Three. If you never get that mixed up, we'll get along great." She did and they didn't, but that's another story. Hard-core. That's the point. Tom is the most hard-core sportsman I've met.

Tom worked in a paper mill, a job he'd chosen because it didn't tax his brains or his body. He could set the machines to run several thousand feet of toilet paper while he read fishing magazines until the end of his shift. Then, fresh as a daisy, Tom would fish for at least six hours before grabbing a little sleep and doing it all over again.

And again and again. Tom fished or hunted virtually every day of the spring, summer, and fall. He only missed a day if monster waves made it utterly impossible to venture out on Lake Michigan. His boat was a 14-foot "car-topper," hardly the typical Great Lakes craft, but Tom could and did go out in all sorts of weather, usually at night.

I joined Tom one May night to fish for brown trout during the smelt spawning run. First I had to work a grueling ten-hour day at the magazine, putting an issue to bed. Woozy though I was, I then drove six hours across Wisconsin to Tom's house near the shores of Lake Michigan. I was whipped when I showed up, but Tom and I got talking about fishing. Before I knew it, it was time to fish.

After launching Tom's boat in the dark, we ran down the shore to a nuclear power plant whose warm discharge water was attracting the smelt that were attracting the browns. It was the most surrealistic place I've ever fished. The nuke plant was huge, and ugly enough to be Darth Vader's summer cottage. To keep terrorists from filching enriched uranium, the plant was surrounded by concertina wire and patrolled by guys with M-16s and attack dogs on leashes. The whole area was lit an urpy color by sodium vapor lights. For reasons I never understood, when a brown trout slashed at a smelt here, it made a spooky phosphorescent glow in the dark water. I assumed the fish were radioactive.

Fishing was sensational. We took a two-man limit of browns from eight to thirteen pounds. I was too preoccupied fighting fish to feel how tired I was, though I came out of the evening with sore arms, tooth cuts all over my hands, and a high odor from all the fish slime.

When the sun came up, we shoved Tom's boat back on top of his truck and headed back home. But Tom was too excited to sleep. He got out his scrapbooks and spent the next several hours narrating the photos. The pictures showed Tom with sturgeon bigger than a man, his Vietnamese girlfriend, Tom machine-gunning sharks in the South Pacific, his hunting dogs, all the big salmon he'd caught, and most of the pheasants and ducks he'd shot. When the last scrapbook was closed, I had relived the high points of the life of a gung-ho sportsman. And it was time to fish again.

The weather had turned nasty. All night long, the skies spat a vicious mix of snow, sleet, and rain at us. I didn't have raingear that would fit over my snowmobile suit, so the suit soaked up water and totally lost its insulating qualities. I was so cold I couldn't fall asleep—and so tired I was hallucinating.

And the fishing had turned as frigid as the weather. When I saw we weren't catching anything, I figured my host would quit fishing. Foolish, naive me! Instead, we fished all night and long into the next morning. Well, that was Tom's style. He was a hard-core angler with a rare chance to showcase his fishing skills for the visiting editor.

Tom talked all night long, but since he was muttering with his faced turned away from the storm, I missed most of what he said. But once I clearly heard him say, "We're not catching anything, but at least you're making a reputation. When I get back to the mill, the guys will know the editor of *Fins and Feathers* is no wimp! He's got *balls* the size of *doorknobs!*"

At the moment I was weaving deliriously in the front of the boat in the most total and exquisite agony I've ever known. And I was praying.

Dear Lord, please send down a lightning bolt. Nothing too dramatic, you understand—just a stiff little tingler that would stun us enough so even Tom might stop fishing. Do it, Lord, and I'll ladle soup to drooling old drunks in mackinaws. Or lepers—hey, I'll wash a bunch of lepers for you! You name it, Lord! Pick your favorite charity, and I'll devote the rest of my life to it. Just get me off this damned lake before I start bawling and begging this nice man to take me home!

The Red Gods Deal a Tough Hand to the Doofus and the Great Pretender

Kurt Schultz has lived in his face long enough to get it good and broken in. Ponder his wrinkles awhile and you can pretty much figure how he acquired them: about a third from years of squinting into harsh weather, a third from hard work, another third from laughing at the human comedy.

Kurt, our elk-hunt outfitter, was laughing good-naturedly when we met him. "Gonna be tough, boys," he said, trying to look sympathetic through his grin. "Until this weather breaks, it's gonna be tough."

The joke of Colorado's record-breaking October heat would have been funnier for Bill Gallea and me had it not threatened our trip. This trip represented a lot of anticipation, money, and time. Now here was Kurt saying the woods were so dry that tippy-toeing in them would raise a deafening racket. Here was Kurt saying the elk were all holed up in cool ravines, sucking mint juleps and not moving *at all*.

Ha, ha, ha! Boy, that's a good one on us!

It had all seemed like the Sure Thing, or as close to it as you get in elk hunting. Kurt runs a superb "drop camp" operation, and the particular camp Bill reserved for us has been Kurt's best producer. Hunters typically leave the Waterbury camp early because they fill their tags and have nothing to do. We'd have 12 days, almost two weeks, to bag an elk and a mule deer apiece. How hard could that be?

We began getting intimations of trouble on the day we showed up at Kurt's place to pack into our camp. All day, the men who'd been hunting the previous week trailed into Kurt's office like whipped puppies. They had great suntans but precious little meat to pack home. "Tough hunting," they grumped. "The woods are so dry that sneaking around in all those aspen leaves is like walking on potato chips."

[Meanwhile, somewhere high above earth, two Red Gods check in to begin their new assignment. They extract a pair of dog-eared manila files from a file cabinet, pour mugs of coffee, and sit down at a table. Their chairs offer an excellent view of the high Colorado Rockies country where Kurt Schultz runs his drop camps.]

RED GOD IZZIE: Clarence, my man! Good to see you. I guess we'll be working together again.

RED GOD CLARENCE: Yeah. Of course, these guys hunt together a lot, so we pull a lot of shared assignments. You and I must have met in, ummm, 1969 wasn't it? When Gallea was teaching Grooms about ruffed grouse.

IZZIE: Sounds about right. We've given the boys some great hunts over the years.

CLARENCE: Well, they're competent, hard-working upland hunters. It's just when they turn to big game that things go queer. My guy, Gallea, is in great shape, and he's a pretty good shot. But Grooms with a big game rifle is a doofus—worse than a joke.

IZZIE: Remember their deer hunt last year?

CLARENCE: I wish I could forget.

IZZIE: What an embarrassment.

CLARENCE: Even worse than the year before.

IZZIE: Which I hadn't thought possible.

Maybe I should tell you how a drop-camp hunt works. Hunters supply their hunting gear, clothing, and food. Kurt has situated a number of camps in prime habitat up in the high country. Each is equipped with a canvas wall tent, some bunks, a wood stove, a propane cook stove, and a table. A biffy is downwind from the tent.

The trip up to your camp is part of the fun. Kurt loads your gear onto his sullen mules, assigns you a horse, and leads the whole train up the steep mountain trail. Knowing that it's bad form, the hunters furtively but fiercely grip their pommels.

Once you're installed in camp, Kurt's wranglers visit every three days to pack down any venison or elk meat you might have hanging in a cool tree. The wranglers checking on us were Sam and Mike. Sam goes six-three, maybe six-four, and that's before he puts on high-heeled cowboy boots and a tall hat, after which he's not much smaller than an elk. And Sam is Kurt's *little* wrangler. Mike's the boy who's got size on him.

While we waited to make our ride up to the camp, a hunter from New York drifted over to the corral where Sam and Mike were tending stock. They noticed his nervous appraisal of the horses but didn't let on.

Sam: So Mike, who you gonna put on *Ol' Terminator?*

Mike: How about the guy from New York?

Sam: Oh man, would *that* be funny!

Later they introduced the New York hunter to the horse he'd ride up the trail. Dusty is a bland bay gelding with a Roman nose who probably wouldn't buck if a screaming cougar pounced on his back. The wranglers gingerly handed over the reins saying, "You look like a guy who can handle a horse. *Steady there, Terminator! Steady!*" I told Kurt I wanted a horse with absolutely no sense of imagination. He reflected, then said, "I got one. Spicy hasn't had an original thought in ten years." Spicy wheezed nonstop on the two-hour trek up to the Waterbury camp. She threatened to lie down and die at any moment. No problem. That's her way. Kurt would only have worried if the old gold brick hadn't wheezed.

On the way up the mountain, we spotted a cow elk with two youngsters. Mama hid behind a little spruce, though she left a lot of elk hanging out on both sides. Apparently not every elk is as smart as a rocket scientist. I began to think it couldn't be *so* hard to bag one of these animals, after all.

RED GOD IZZIE: So what are we planning for the boys this year?

RED GOD CLARENCE: Suit yourself with Grooms. As for Gallea, I don't figure I'll owe him an elk for maybe 40 or 50 years.

IZZIE: You sound testy, Clarence. Are you harboring a wee bit of a grudge?

CLARENCE: You got that right. I probably never told you about his first bull, about four years ago. Get this: Gallea goes on stand on the first morning of his first elk hunt. I let him wait a whole 15 minutes, then I run three raghorn bulls out in front of him. It was cute. His eyes just about bugged out of his head. Next thing, the woods start drumming with hooves like the cavalry is coming. Out come five bulls! Five *legal* bulls. They commence to run around in a circle in the open like a damned elk carousel.

IZZIE: Man, you were being generous!

CLARENCE: You know how it is. Stunts like that are half the fun of being a Red God. Anyway, I stop this one five-point bull right in front of him, broadside, just over a hundred yards. Of course, he drops it. Even *Grooms* could have hit that one.

IZZIE: Mighty generous.

CLARENCE: That's not what gripes me. So I gave him an easy bull . . . hey, it was good for giggles. But next thing I know, Gallea's telling everybody that the secret to successful elk hunting is using "Minnesota deer-hunting techniques"! Can you believe it? He's hunted elk for *15 minutes* and he's coming on like *Jim Effing Zumbo!* I make him the world's luckiest elk hunter and he's ready to star in an instructional video!

IZZIE: Incredible. Hunters are incredible. After all my years as a Red God, I find I still can't underestimate them. But if I know you, Clarence, you didn't get mad; you got even.

CLARENCE: Oh yeah. I jerked him back to earth pretty good the next time he hunted elk. With me, Gallea's deep in debt. Will be for years.

IZZIE: Well, it's going to be a hard-luck camp all around then, because I'm not giving Grooms any breaks. I mean, he comes into this camp at 10,000 feet with the aerobic conditioning of Santa Claus. In this thin air, it's going to be a monumental task for him to hike out of the tent.

As Kurt had promised, the hunting was hard. Frankly, *breathing* was hard at that altitude—for me, at least. Having sampled both types, I know I prefer air with oxygen in it. Everything on a mountain is slanty, so walking there is like hiking around on the roof of a house. And if you have to ascend a ridge, it's more like climbing a ladder with a plastic bag over your head.

My step was not made more buoyant by the fact that I was toting a nine-pound rifle and packing a massive amount of gear for disassembling my victims. At least I was clever enough to lighten my topographical map by trimming away all the parts showing terrain so far away I'd never reach it, which was 98 percent of the map.

I could usually walk about 80 yards before my lungs gave out and I had to hang on an aspen and wheeze. Then I'd go for another 80 before stopping to suck wind, desperately seeking air with traces of oxygen in it. I told myself I was "still-hunting," though anyone watching me might have called it Panting All Over the Mountain.

Not that our choice of hunting technique made a difference. *Nothing* made a difference. We still-hunted, faster-hunted, and stood on stand. We hunted above camp, below camp, and to the left and right of camp. We hunted aspens, dark timber, game trails, water holes, and parks. We hunted early, late, and noon-ish.

It didn't matter. We weren't seeing deer. We weren't seeing elk. We weren't seeing crap.

Each evening, Bill and I would get together back at camp to discuss our day's adventures. It didn't take long.

"See anything?"

"No. You?"

"No."

"So . . . what's for dinner?"

The absence of game was understandable in view of the summer-like heat. With the simple faith of ungulates, the elk had believed the calendar instead of the thermometer, so they had all donned thick winter coats, though it felt like August. Clearly, elk weren't going to travel in that sultry air except in an air-conditioned vehicle. I could understand that. What had me discouraged was the total absence of game sign. It was hard to believe there were any elk on our mountain.

"I've been wondering, Bill."

"Yeah?"

"I know heat can stop the elk from moving. But we're not seeing any fresh droppings. Can heat stop elk from shitting?"

RED GOD IZZIE: After last year's fiasco, it makes my heart sing to see Grooms suffering so much.

RED GOD CLARENCE: My guy's killing himself. Yesterday, Gallea walked almost to the bottom of the mountain and hunted all the way up those ridges where mountain goats are afraid to go. Today he fought his way into Hell's Gulch and back. That's a jungle. In spite of myself, I'm starting to feel sorry for him.

IZZIE [in a sing-song voice]: Maybe he should try the Minnesota deer-hunting technique. I hear that never fails.

CLARENCE: That pretentious prick! We'll keep the weather just where it is.

The torrid weather that was killing our hunting made for wonderful camping. In that thin air, the high Rockies were stunningly beautiful. Everything was sharp-edged and color-saturated like Kodachrome underexposed half a stop. Golden eagles cleaved effortless paths through the intensely blue sky. You could point a camera in any direction—eyes shut, even—and get a picture pretty enough for the Sierra Club Calendar. I was startled one day to notice how vivid and detailed the Roquefort cheese moon was as it hung overhead at noon. Well, why not? I was a heckuva lot closer to the moon than I'd ever been before, and I no longer had to peer through earth's atmosphere to see it.

I liked everything about our camp except the reading material we found there. We heard some camps had copies of the current *Playboy.* Ours had a bulky tome called *Report of the President's Council on Competitiveness,* representing some of Dan Quayle's best economic thinking. But it was mighty slow going, with a bunch of turgid sentences between the juicy parts. Yet that's not why I was disappointed. You ever try to start a *fire* with a President's Council Report? What with the thick paper and all that soggy writing, a presidential report burns like wet cardboard. Now, you take a *Playboy* with its thin, crumply paper . . . just a couple pages will get a campfire burning lustily.

Halfway through our hunt, Bill and I began running into Jim. A pleasant fellow with an elfish grin and long legs, Jim was hunting out of a camp in the adjoining drainage system. He liked to walk. Soon Bill and I couldn't go anywhere without seeing Jim or Jim's tracks. Jim wasn't seeing deer, elk, or game sign, either. He believed all the game had migrated to Montana or somewhere else cool.

Jim told Bill how his partners shot what he figured was the last elk on the mountain. Of six hunters in his camp, five had VCR cameras. Two were filming some cow elk in a meadow when in their viewfinders there appeared an elk sporting antlers. They dropped cameras, grabbed rifles, and dropped the young bull.

Two days later, their outfitter came up to pack out their elk. (Bill and I later learned he was an outlaw operator illegally running hunts on Kurt's turf.) The outfitter was concerned about one horse in his string that had never packed meat before. Strapping bloody meat to an inexperienced horse can panic the animal, because it smells the blood and decides *it* is bleeding. When the horse learns it can't run away from the bloody smell, the usual result is a colossal screw-up.

"You guys got Vick's Vaporub?" the outfitter asked. Nobody did. "If you put a little Vaporub on a horse, he won't smell the meat," he explained.

"Well, I got some Ben Gay," somebody offered.

The outfitter smeared a big dollop of Ben Gay on the horse's upper lip. Ben Gay *stings*. The poor animal freaked out and reared up with a scream that shattered rocks. Because of the weight of the elk meat, the horse kept right on going over backward, cracking its head on a boulder and knocking itself out. At the sight of his horse upside down with four legs twitching in the air, the outfitter went ballistic. "My fucking horse! My fucking horse! Someone get a knife and cut loose my fucking horse!"

All of this is documented. Five purring VCR cameras caught the whole scene.

RED GOD CLARENCE: Poor Gallea. He's really busting his buns.

RED GOD IZZIE: I know. For nine days our boys've been rolling nothing but gutter balls.

CLARENCE: It's hard to keep a grudge, even against the Great Pretender, when he keeps trying so hard.

IZZIE: I'm considering running an animal past my Doofus. Panting that hard, he couldn't hit it anyway.

CLARENCE: It might be time to lighten up on the boys a little.

IZZIE: If nothing else, I'm getting bored. Let's show our guys some new weather.

Our trip was almost over when milky streaks began appearing in the seamless cobalt sky. Soon great fat flakes of snow began tumbling down like so many crystal doilies. The snowfall increased until our mountain landscape resembled the inside of a snow globe. When snow smothered the potato-chip aspen leaves, the crunchy woods became suddenly and eerily silent, and I felt I'd stepped into a movie with no sound track.

And still the snow came, scarcely letting up for three days. The spruces and lodgepole pines loaded up with snow. Snow stuck in patches on the black bark of dark timber. At one point, I looked around and groaned, "Oy vay! I've seen this scene before. This looks exactly like a Bev Doolittle painting. If I look sharp, I'm gonna see the frontiersman on the appaloosa."

Then it seemed like the snow started to mix with powdered crystals of big game animals, rehydrating them into life. We began spotting animals.

Bill sneaked his way right into a small herd of elk. They were feeding so intently they didn't notice. After all, they hadn't ventured out to eat for at least nine days. Bill would have had a "gimme" shot if any had been legal, which they were not.

One afternoon, I sauntered into a gang of mule deer that were almost close enough to touch. With adrenaline flooding my belly, I studied each of their heads in turn. Alas, all were does. One gave me the evil eye for a long time before deciding I was either the ugliest tree she'd ever seen or a hunter with no doe permit.

On the second storm day, I went on stand in a little castle of pink rocks that some previous hunter had built. I kept getting dozy, but I didn't want to nap because my hopes were high. Game was afoot! I invented techniques to keep alert. I made little snowmen. When I still felt sleepy, I began making snow-women with exciting physiques. Eat your heart out, Dolly, you poor flat-chested gal.

Though we were getting close to game, we weren't getting any gun play. Bill played peek-a-boo with a cow and bull that never quite offered him a shot. I spent half an hour watching a bull feeding beyond the range of my .270 in a rock-strewn bowl where I had no chance to stalk him. He was an old patriarch with so much beam length he could have scratched his butt with the tip of his rack.

Once I peered over a ridge and found myself right on top of three mule deer. Two were bucks, one probably legal. That deer carried so much rack he almost surely had the requisite three points to a side, but he bolted before I could count points. I didn't want to fire at an "almost" surely legal animal.

RED GOD CLARENCE: You gotta admit, the boys are conducting themselves with a little class. I've about decided to give Gallea one slim chance to score.

RED GOD IZZIE: My Doofus is so serious about hunting he even left his stinky cigars down the mountain with Kurt. Grooms doesn't *deserve* anything this year, but it'd be a hoot to run a good bull by him . . . to see if he shoots or just loads up his shorts.

On my last day of hunting, I was walking through a winter wonderland of snowy woods when I saw what looked like mule-deer ears off to my left. Drawing upon my extensive familiarity with deer anatomy, I reasoned, "Gee, if those are ears, the rest of the deer can't be far away." I raised my rifle three times to get a better look through my scope.

Steve to Scope: Ears! I see ears! Check it out, Scope!

Scope to Steve: False alarm, big guy. Those are leaves.

Steve to Scope: Look again, Scope. I swear I see ears.

Scope to Steve [rather sarcastically]: S-o-r-r-y.

Steve to Scope [vehemently]: Scope, we had this same discussion three years ago in Wisconsin. Please look again, *dammit!*

Scope to Steve: No, it's just . . . hey, Steve, you're not gonna *believe* this: I see ears! I see eyes and . . . hot damn, I see antlers! *It's a legal buck!* BUST THE SUCKER!"

Just then an Engleman's spruce received one snowflake too many—the straw that broke the camel's back, as it were—and the tree dumped its cargo of snow. Snow slid off the treetop, crashed down on lower clumps, and triggered a frosty avalanche exactly between me and the deer. Moments later, with only a few snowflakes still winking earthward, I could see again. The buck was lurching to his feet. I snapped off a quick shot.

On stand behind a deadfall overlooking a big meadow, Bill saw an elk step up over the ridge. Then another. And another. Alas, he was looking at a cow, a spike, and a raghorn. Nothing legal. Ahh, but what was that animal feeding furtively in the shade of the spruces? Wasn't that one sporting headgear?

Bill watched. And watched. The sun passed behind the far mountain range. Light began draining out of the opalescent sky.

Bill studied the rack with increasing desperation as the end of legal shooting hours closed in on him. His license was valid for a four-point bull or better. "There are obviously two points on the end of each beam," Bill concluded after the ten longest minutes of his life. "But I'll be damned if I can tell if there are two brow tines on a side or just one. Who'd believe it could be so tough to *count to four?*"

Back at camp the next day, Bill and I solemnly clinked tin cups and toasted his bull with the last precious ounces of our Scotch supply.

"Here's to elk hunting and good friends," I said.

"To elk hunting, good friends, *and* the generosity of the Red Gods," said Bill.

RED GOD CLARENCE: Awww! Isn't that sweet?

RED GOD IZZIE: Don't let it go to your head, Clarence. He's just speaking metaphorically.

Bill licked the last trace of Scotch off his lips. He was pensive, serene, totally mellow. "Well," he said, "the old Minnesota deer-hunting technique scores again."

ABOUT THE AUTHOR

If you've just finished reading *The Ones That Got Away*, you already know more about Steve Grooms than any human being should decently know about another. However, for the record:

While his hunting and fishing career has had its ups and downs, his writing has been consistently outstanding. Grooms has written about nature and the outdoors for a number of years, and he is the former editor of *Fins and Feathers*, a magazine devoted to outdoor sports. He's the author of two previous titles published by NorthWord Press, *Bluebirds!* and *The Cry of the Sandhill Crane*. Both are lively, informative natural history volumes about intriguing birds. *The Ones That Got Away* is a bit different; its tone is personal, provocative, self-effacing, and FUNNY.

Steve lives in St. Paul, Minnesota, with his wife Kathe and their wild-about-animals daughter Molly. The family travels frequently to their recreational property on the shores of Lake Superior.

What's next for Grooms? As of this writing, he's working on a book about timber wolves to be published by NorthWord in 1993.

For more outdoor humor
from NorthWord Press and Willow Creek Press,
be sure to ask at your favorite bookstore for the
"feverishly funny" books of Bruce Cochran:

For more serious reading about the outdoors,
ask for these fine NorthWord / Willow Creek titles:

 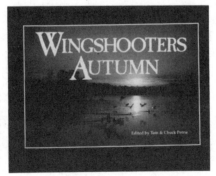 

Published by NorthWord Press, Inc.
P.O. Box 1360 / Minocqua, WI 54548

For a free catalog of NorthWord products, call
1-800-336-5666